D0447127

The Cowgirl and the Racehorse

THE
COWGIRL
AND THE
RACEHORSE

A Recovery

Ashley Wells

Lantern Publishing & Media ● Brooklyn, NY

2020
Lantern Publishing & Media
128 Second Place
Brooklyn, NY 11231
www.lanternpm.org

Copyright © 2020 Ashley Wells

All rights reserved. No part of this book may be reproduced, stored in a retrieval system, or transmitted in any form or by any means, electronic, mechanical, photocopying, recording, or otherwise, without the written permission of Lantern Publishing & Media.

Printed in the United States of America

Library of Congress Cataloging-in-Publication Data

Names: Wells, Ashley, author.
Title: The cowgirl and the racehorse : a recovery / Ashley Wells.
Description: Brooklyn, NY : Lantern Publishing & Media, 2020. | Includes
     bibliographical references.
Identifiers: LCCN 2020028992 (print) | LCCN 2020028993 (ebook) | ISBN
     9781590566336 (paperback) | ISBN 9781590566343 (ebook)
Subjects: LCSH: Wells, Ashley. | Horsemanship—United States—Biography. |
     Human-animal relationships. | Horsemanship—Safety measures. | Race
     houses—Training.
Classification: LCC SF309 .W44 2020 (print) | LCC SF309 (ebook) | DDC
     798.2—dc23
LC record available at https://lccn.loc.gov/2020028992
LC ebook record available at https://lccn.loc.gov/2020028993

Contents

Rebel

AFTER I LOST Shoshona, my horse of thirteen years, the grief weighed on me, weakening my bones. I imagined my ribs as bird bones, unsubstantial and frail, wrapped around my organs—the vital parts of me. An ache and a homesickness set in that I wasn't able to shake or outrun. At the time, I wasn't ready to take on another horse of my own but needed to somehow reconnect with horses, to feel their pulsing speed and their quiet stillness, their rhythm and their strength. So I sought out riding partners.

After meeting online through an ad she had placed in a horse forum, Jennifer and I began riding her horses, Cody and Rebel, each week from her Coarsegold, California, home on the top of a mountain. We'd meander through the trails blazed by spindly-legged deer, whom we would spot sometimes, their delicate ears barely poking through the wisps of weeds and brush. As we moved up and down hills, under the low-swooping branches, along fences bordering her neighbors' homes peppered across the mountain, we talked for hours. Despite her being twenty-three years older, we immediately connected, realizing during those rides that we wanted some of the same things out of life—the freedom to wander with our horses, to be powerful and strong with them, to have a relationship with them. We wanted each day to have those magical moments when everything is tender and loving—those moments when a horse drops her head for you to rub her face, when she looks you in the eye and everything just stops.

Trail riding felt uncomplicated and pure until my fall. After we mounted our horses, I on Cody and Jennifer on Rebel, I noticed that my stirrups were too short, preventing me from being properly balanced in the saddle. But I dismissed this, thinking I would be fine. I had been riding for over twenty years after all. I now realize how arrogant I had been in thinking that even out on the trail, it being defined by its unpredictability, I could control the situation. I also see that this moment was keenly indicative of the way I treated myself at that time in my life. Despite the danger in riding while imbalanced, I still did it, unwilling to cause a fuss by stopping to adjust the stirrups—even in service of self-preservation—and downplaying the risk in my own head. And I paid for it.

Cody's stride was quick and energetic as we left Jennifer's property and moved further away from her house. Although a forward-moving stride is good in a horse, Cody's was hurried, rushed. It just didn't feel right. About an hour into our ride, we neared a hill covered in a blanket of dry, crisp-looking brush. Jennifer and Rebel climbed it first. Rebel's strong haunches propelled them up the steep hill, making it look easy. I did little to prepare Cody or myself for the ascent. I did not insist that Cody stop and get with me before we began our own climb, nor did I ensure that he was under me and was collected. Before I knew it, he surged into a gallop. As he barreled up the hill, he bucked, kicking out with his right rear leg. This combination of movements and the lack of a correct seat launched me over Cody's left shoulder.

I heard Jennifer yell, "No!" from up ahead, and all I could see was a flash of Cody's shoulder as I struggled to lift my arms in front of my face to break my fall.

Failing to get my arms up fast enough, I hit the ground headfirst. My face scraped against the rough earth and the brittle weeds before my body seemed to collapse on itself. I remember rolling and then sitting up immediately despite being completely hazy, as though all of the trees and rocks had lost their hard edges. Blinking a couple of times, I attempted to clear away the fog, to place myself in my body again. As Jennifer crouched in front of me, a glint of worry crossed her face, and I knew something was wrong.

Searching for the source of Jennifer's concern, I touched my face—heat was radiating across my right cheek. My fingers were covered with blood and dirt. But the blood on my face didn't scare me nearly as much as the thought of internal bleeding. Pain ripped through my body, from my neck through to my ribs and back, and I felt cold all over. Sweat rolled down my face, filling the long scrape across my cheek and dripping into my split lip, stinging and burning.

Since we were so far out on the trail, we had to either walk or ride back. There was no way I could climb back onto Cody so I attempted to walk, leading him beside me. Slowly, we worked our way through the brush and dirt, but each time Cody ducked his head to pick off a chunk of grass, it was as if my ribs were being torn apart. My stomach churned and nausea took hold. I simply couldn't go any further, and I surely couldn't make it up the mountain to Jennifer's house.

After propping me against a large rock in the shade, Jennifer found a corral in a neighbor's pasture and put Rebel in before hopping on Cody. Within minutes, she and Cody disappeared through the trees and hills. Sitting there alone, watching Rebel pace and paw, I was certain that I would die—certain that my insides were filling with blood. To stave off the panic, I focused on steadying myself by taking measured, shallow breaths, because the deep, satisfying ones were impossible in my state. A trail of ants climbed up the rock in a neat line, and I watched them, counting each tiny, black body.

The doctor gave me clear instructions not to get back on a horse until after the surgery to fill my fractured vertebrae with cement and stabilize my spine. During my time out of the saddle, I struggled to sort through both fear and the compulsion to ride again—a strange and unnerving combination. In all of my prior training and in all of the cowgirl narratives I devoured growing up—the movies I watched until I had them memorized, the cowgirl songs I hummed around the barn, the stories I read as truth—the same enduring cliché reverberated throughout: If you fall off, you must get back in the saddle. According to these narratives, the newly born fear that I harbored didn't matter. All that mattered was that I get back on.

—

This is the story of love between a girl and her horse—the story of the cowgirl. When I was young, I wrote detective stories that I carried around in a briefcase, adding to them obsessively. Inspired by the Nancy Drew books my grandmother bought me from an antique shop, my stories were centered likewise on a young detective, except that mine had a horse. She consulted with the horse and often got out of trouble by galloping off into the sunset. My detective stories somehow evolved into orphan tales of inexplicably terrible things happening to a young girl's home and family and of her racing out to pasture, jumping on the back of her silver mare, and escaping to live in the woods, safe and alone with her horse.

Often, in my stories, a fire would destroy the house with the entire family in it, and our heroine would barely escape with her life. Sometimes murderers would break in late at night, terrorizing the family isolated in their country home, but the girl would sneak out through her window, creep shoeless through the brambles and weeds to her horse's pasture, climb on, grab hold of the horse's inky-black mane, gallop full speed toward the fence, clear it and flee—just the two of them. In these stories, the horse protected the girl, kept her warm at night, and thus made her powerful and capable of existing in a scary world.

—

Ever since I can remember, I've been hyper-aware of violence—more specifically, of the threat of violence. The day my father found a dead body in the lake while he was fishing, I realized that the world wasn't safe. I was very young then—maybe five—and had crept into the hallway, clutching my little gray kitten, to listen to my father tell my mother what had happened. Warm light spilled from the living room into the hallway where I stood motionless against the wall. He had been fishing up in northern California, a few hours from our home, when he spotted what appeared to be a log near the shore of the lake, water lapping against it. When he got nearer, though, he realized that it was actually a dingy navy-blue sleeping bag in a mound. Rusted chains were tangled around it, and a small hand peeked out from underneath. From my parents' conversation, the word *mutilated* stuck with me the most, although I didn't know exactly what it meant. I had gathered enough to imagine a pale body, mouth agape, eyes and other body parts missing.

Growing up in the country, I loved the aloneness and the space. I loved the freedom to run and roam. Instead of playing hide-and-seek in the house like my friends did, my father, brother, and I played among the seemingly endless orchards. Shoshona and I would often set off, completely alone, down the narrow farm roads and canals behind our home. But I was also aware, at least in some vague sense, that my family's seclusion meant vulnerability as well. I became certain of this when, late one night, I woke to distant sounds of men shouting and the sinister crunch of metal. The deep, menacing voices traveled the way sound does in the country. Peering from my bedroom window, I made out a group of figures standing between the trees, their shadows stretched long across the earth. They were yelling into the orchards. I saw what looked like bats in their hands. One man held his in the air—proudly—as if it were a flag. I woke my parents, and they looked out from the safety of our yard. Our Yellow Lab, Buck, barked and frantically ran the fence line, his massive paws pounding at the ground. My parents called the police and were assured that the sheriff would be on his way soon.

By the time the sheriff finally arrived, the men had already retreated, leaving in their wake the charred skeleton of my neighbor's car parked in the orchard. I don't know what happened or why, but once again picking up details through eavesdropping on my parents, I learned that the teenaged son of our neighbor was driven off the country road that ran between his home and mine by the group of men. The boy ran and hid in the trees while the men proceeded to destroy his car and set it aflame. On one of my trail rides in the following week, Shoshona and I ambled by the place. All that was left of the incident was a dark outline of ash in the dirt where the burned car had stood.

I knew I should be afraid, sitting there on my horse and looking down at the site where violence and fear were so clearly drawn on the earth, yet I wasn't. Certainly not the way I was as I lay in my bed late at night or when I heard my parents repeat rumors of gang violence leaking from cities into the country. My father, an avid hunter skilled with a gun, took my mother, brother, and me to the gun range to take classes on how to shoot. We learned that if someone broke into our home, we should run and crouch between the bed and the wall, guns clenched in our hands and aimed at the door. We learned that we should wait for the intruder to come through the doorway. We learned that we should pull the trigger then. In those moments, I was afraid. But I was never afraid on Shoshona. With cowgirl stories buried in my brain, I imagined myself like those heroines—plucky and adventurous, galloping away from danger on my brave steed, positive that I was untouchable as long as I was on Shoshona. Although she was such a large animal, unpredictable and imposing, I felt safe. Had I been walking on the ground by myself, I would have been vulnerable and scared out there. But riding Shoshona, I was strong and fast. This is important.

—

In my more than twenty years of riding experience before the fall, I had never worried about being seriously injured, though I understood that horses were undeniably dangerous. I had heard the horror stories of broken bones and even death. Almost every equestrian I knew had one such story. In fact, the story of the rodeo cowgirl is inextricably linked with these horrors. Women in the West rode and ranched alongside the men, so naturally, they burst into rodeo atop their horses when the horses took off. However, this was not without the resentment of more urban audiences.

When rodeo star Bonnie McCarroll died tragically after being dragged by a bronco in 1929, her death was cited as a reason to ban women from rodeo altogether, despite the fact that men, too, faced similar fates. McCarroll had had close calls before, evidenced by an iconic 1915 photo featuring her landing directly on her head, but she wouldn't give up the rush of rodeo life. The rough-and-tumble rodeo cowgirl was shoved to the sidelines and given two choices: barrel racing or rodeo queen. So, she could either zip around three barrels set in a cloverleaf pattern or represent rodeo itself, but she wouldn't compete with the men.

In her book *Rodeo Queens and the American Dream*, Joan Burbick untangles the history of rodeo in the West, the whitewashing and colonization by settlers in that region, the cruelty as well as the glitz. She notes that until the 1950s, Indigenous women were frequently crowned rodeo queens, although you wouldn't know it from pop culture. As rodeo started to be framed as part of our national mythology, it was largely white middle-class women who were charged with representing and promoting the sport while white men competed for glory and prizes. According to Burbick, promoters "repeated nonstop the tired clichés of how rodeo reflected ranching and America's heroic pioneer past" (52). The story of the West became equated with the story of the cowboy. With that, the horse came to symbolize freedom, and both came to represent American*ness*, with the horse acting as a kind of shorthand for Freedom (capital "F")—"that American construct made up of equal parts Manifest Destiny, grit, hubris, and blindness" (Holbrook Pierson, 145). The rodeo queens and cowgirls, decked out in rhinestones and chaps, carved out a place for themselves in both rodeo and the Hollywood Western.

Running beneath all of this is a dark undercurrent—from colonization to the ways we treat horses, cattle, and the land. Animals are routinely dominated for sport and sponsorships. Currently, wild horses, the very symbol of freedom that we love to exalt, are under attack and subject to brutal roundups by the Bureau of Land Management. If we choose not to look closely at how horses, sheep, and cows have been exploited as part of the colonizers' drive westward, their stories form compelling narratives of man, woman, and animal in symbiosis. Beginning with the charismatic stars of Wild West shows and rodeo, the cowgirl narrative has taken many forms, all reproducing for an audience the relationship between girl and horse. And girls, horseless or otherwise, have gobbled these stories up because they hold a kernel of truth and desire. They stir in us something raw and elemental.

My father is distrustful of horses and their lingering wildness, and he takes every opportunity to remind me of the terrifying injuries and mayhem they've been known to cause. He is generally a courageous man, street-savvy and well versed in the ways of the world. He can anticipate what a man might do or think, but he cannot do that with a horse, and this fact unnerves him. Yet, despite all of this, and despite my own brushes with near harm, before the fall I simply had never felt afraid the way I did afterwards. I certainly never thought that I would fear being in the saddle like I feared the world outside of it. Still, a need to ride again continued to nag at me, as did a strong unwillingness to redefine myself, to renegotiate the identity I had carved out for myself as a horsewoman.

One of my earliest memories in the saddle was on an Appaloosa named Popcorn. It took place after a family barbeque, when I was five. My grandmother, aunt, and mother were there. I know others were, too—my grandfather, father, and brother—but they don't readily appear in the memory. After lifting me into the saddle, my grandmother wrapped a thick leather belt around my waist and the horn, a move that in hindsight I realize was incredibly dangerous, regardless of her good intentions. The image branded in my mind centers on me being perched atop old spotted Popcorn, my mother, aunt, and grandmother surrounding us, ready to stop him should he try to walk off or spook. In that moment, these women were forging a path for me, a path they themselves had already begun to explore.

My abiding love for horses was birthed in that quiet moment as I sat tall on Popcorn, but it was solidified when I was eight years old and Shoshona entered my life. She had belonged to my aunt Erika before my mother bought her for me. From the first moment I saw Shoshona, I was in love with her pale, gray coat sprinkled with flecks of brown; with her deep-black mane and tail; with the heft of her muscles, the weight of her body, and the ease of her movements. She was the kind of horse I saw in the movies. Sitting on her back, my feet barely reaching the middle of her round stomach, with my grandmother and mother looking on, I was secure and powerful. Free, yet completely at home.

———

When we were kids, my brother played hockey at our local ice rink. As I watched him breeze around the rink, I felt a burning jealousy and yearned to try it myself, despite my heavy involvement in my own hobbies. My mother, who always encouraged us to try new things, signed me up. As I stood in the musky equipment room, the faint smell of sweat hanging in the air, my new coach held the cumbersome shoulder pads over my head before lowering them and tightening the strings around my chest. While he outfitted me in my pads, I tried not to let on that I was worried about being the only girl on the ice.

Sliding onto the ice was freeing, even with those heavy pads, which, to my surprise, allowed me to skate with abandon, unafraid of falling or crashing. As I sped around the rink during warm-up, the cool air made my face tingle while the sweat collected under my helmet, matting my hair. The red and blue lines painted beneath the ice blurred as I zoomed around. I loved playing hockey, especially the speed and the freedom to be asser-tive in a way that wasn't typically acceptable for a young girl. But hockey created a conflict in my schedule as horse show season approached, along with the spring weather, and I was forced to choose. It wasn't a *real* choice, though, because of course I would choose the horse shows. I had already invested so much of not only my time but also that of my mother, aunt, grandmother, and trainer—the team of women who molded and shaped me. If Shoshona had not been part of the process and the reason for such rigid discipline—frequent riding, competitions, daily stall-cleaning, grooming, and deep-set aches and pains from training—I doubt I would have stuck with it. The horse was the key—a conduit. I could afford to give up the confidence I had gained from hockey because I already had it with Shoshona—in more nuanced and vivid ways.

I was seventeen when my great-grandmother had a stroke. She was already blind, and the stroke left her completely unable to care for herself, so my parents put her in a convalescent home near my high school. Each day after school, I sat by her bed, reading to her, holding her tiny hand, and applying balm to her cracked, dry lips. Performing these actions with a sort of religious devotion, I stayed with her even when it seemed like too much for a seventeen-year-old girl.

When Shoshona grew old, with legs too creaky and unsure to carry me, I cared for her with the same sense of loyalty and dedication. Often, I would visit the ranch and just stand in the pasture with her, my hand resting on her shoulder, which remained strong and sturdy even then.

Watching the other horses in her pasture graze until the sky turned pink and listening to the world around me—the slow movements of the horses chewing, their hooves gliding through the grass, their content sighs—gave me something that my life apart from Shoshona could not. Out there, I found a sense of peace and connectivity that I couldn't find elsewhere. That I still can't find elsewhere.

And I'm not alone in this. Most horsewomen in my life have described similar experiences: their own moments of stability, strength, and peace. From the cowboy stories about men wandering across wide ranges on their horses, I know that men are capable of feeling this connection, too. I know that they must, but I haven't met any who do aside from a few of the horsemanship trainers I've studied with. Mainly, I hear men speak of their horses in terms that signal an entirely different relationship, one centered upon work or notoriety. Simply put, there is something about girls and horses.

Horses and humans have been interconnected for millennia, but this love affair between women and horses is a more modern phenomenon. When men were through using them for war, status, and transportation, horses were left to the women, who rode forth with passion and gusto. Throughout time and culture, the image of the woman has vacillated between the unruly one who needs to be bridled and subdued and the benevolent mother figure who nurtures and gives. One way or another, our womanhood has been symbolically associated with the natural world, which has been treated as exploitable. Communion with nature through our horses gives us a chance to tap into a hidden strength by allowing us to claim our feminine history as our own.

"Women, who are identified with nature," Ynestra King writes, "have been similarly objectified and subordinated in patriarchal society" (471). When we ride, we subvert all of that, feeling the rhythms of the Amazons, of horse goddesses and the like, "already more like horses than [we] know" (Holbrook Pierson, 162). In a world where women are still marginalized, this is an opportunity we aren't often afforded outside of the saddle. The benefits outweigh the dangers of riding and interacting with an animal who can be at times flighty and unpredictable; fear and undeniable attraction are thus allowed to exist at once.

While in Arizona for a horsemanship clinic, I drove with a couple of other female attendees from the trainer's forty-five-acre ranch to the nearest town to shop and eat lunch. As Candace, Rachel, and I crossed the desert, passing through the broad nothingness, the subject of girls and horses came up. The conversation led to a discussion of why we see more women than men with horses, and why young girls often start out being loving and gentle with their horses before falling into a very different relationship—an odd arrangement that hinges upon control, domination, and attachment. Candace and I had talked about this before. We had speculated but could never arrive at any clear answers. We agreed that it begins with the prominence of traditional forms of horsemanship that rely on dominance and submission. They were all we knew, all we had access to, growing up. What we couldn't figure out, though, is how girls make that shift. How do we reconcile the act of removing all of our horses' options except for submission with the fact that we, too, have been bridled in so many ways? I had been one of those girls myself, yet I still couldn't really explain it. Cowgirls challenge the patriarchy in some ways but reproduce it in others, and the animals continue to lose.

Rachel sat quietly for a moment before tucking her dark hair behind her ears. "I feel like a lot of it has to do with fear," she said. "We start out totally unafraid. When we were little girls, we jumped on our horses bareback with just a rope halter and rode around wherever. As we get older, we get all this baggage. It makes us afraid."

As I listened to Rachel, goosebumps crawled across my skin. Finally, someone voiced what I had been troubled by. I knew deep down that the fear mattered, and after my fall the fear came to matter more as I struggled to rekindle my relationship with the fearless girl I once was. It wasn't so simple as "If you fall off, get back on." Not anymore.

Shoshona

TREASURE STOMPED IMPATIENTLY as the cranio-sacral therapist, Shea, gently worked her fingers all over his head. Everything was silent. It was still early, so it was just the three of us in Treasure's stall amid the gray of morning. Despite the chill that numbed my fingers, Shea's were nimble and precise, finding the exact spots where the bone and muscle compressions needed to be released—lingering evidence of Treasure's former life as a racehorse. Slowly, we would erase all traces of an existence that was filled with stress and scarcity. Slowly, starting with his bones and his guts, we would convince Treasure that he was a new horse, a different horse.

Treasure fought Shea's holds at first. He was unsure of the change in energy and twisted his great, long neck out of her hands, lifting his head high above her own, far beyond her reach. Shea quietly persisted, and he relaxed into it, settling into the gentle charge of her work—into the relief. Treasure's eyes began to droop as he lazily licked and chewed, emitting soft coos with each breath.

Shea called it the perfect bone. "The maxilla," she said, slowly drawing the syllables out—graceful and lilting. I had seen the skull of a horse, but I had never stopped to consider which bone might be the best of them all. However, I believed Shea unwaveringly because the way she touched Treasure's face so tenderly, so intimately, moving ever so slightly the bones beneath the skin, was sincere. She touched him in a way that I know he had never been touched at the track.

I couldn't help but think of my own bones as Shea said this. I am nearly always thinking about my own bones. While the compression fracture in my spine was filled with cement years ago, my vertebrae still feel shoddy with the constant aches and creaks—reminders of the imperfection beneath my skin. In the years following my surgery, my back has become less and less my own each time a different set of hands danced across it and someone said, "Oh yes, here," stopping where the muscle shivered under their fingers.

The chronic pain acts as a steadfast reminder of the very literal risk of very real injuries and fatalities involved in riding horses, but also of the symbolic and complicated relationship between risk and identity, inspiring contemplation of why I am so compelled to continue riding despite the ever-present, clear, and serious danger. Ultimately, though, my fall revealed a truth that I had been blind to in my more than twenty years of riding: We must shift our way of relating to horses—to all animals. Grappling with this, I've come closer to understanding why so many of the horsewomen I know have had serious accidents and still continue to ride; why I am willing, in adulthood, to wholeheartedly embrace this lifestyle and identity; why the back of a horse feels like home to me.

I haven't always had the vocabulary or insight to understand horsemanship as I do now. I didn't always understand the significant ways that it steadied me through adolescence and shaped my personality into adulthood, influencing the trajectory of my life. I haven't always been so sure. When I was seventeen, I wandered far from home, but Shoshona kept me tethered. She kept me from becoming hopelessly lost, from drifting so far away that I might not return, although I came close. Perhaps this is why I am now so apt to allow my identity as a horsewoman to bleed into my life outside of the arena—why it's so wholly unavoidable that I do.

—

David played in a popular local punk band, and we met through mutual friends. He was a few years older and possessed a swagger and confidence that the boys at my high school seemed to lack. The first night he called me, we spoke on the phone for hours, long after my parents and brothers had gone to sleep. The house stood silent except for the faint whispers coming from my room. The next morning, I woke up blurry-eyed and exhausted, telling my mother I was sick and would need to miss school that day. At lunchtime, I called my best friend at school and excitedly recounted the night before.

During one of our late-night phone conversations a few weeks later, David said he needed to tell me something. He told me that he loved me. Surprised and sure that I didn't love him back, that I didn't even know how to articulate feelings like that, I told him I wasn't ready. This set him off, and he cried into the phone. He told me that he couldn't be with me unless I said it back, that I *had* to say it back. It being my first relationship, I had nothing to compare it to, but this still seemed wrong. I felt trapped. Having never been faced with such dramatic emotions, I said the words back in hopes that it would ease him down and buy me some time to figure things out. It worked, and we went back to the lighthearted and youthful way we had been before. I still don't understand why I didn't simply end it there. Growing up, I had extinguished minor crushes for far less. I don't understand what had changed. To this day, I am disgusted even thinking about it.

That year, I quit student government despite having been junior class president the year before. I ditched school with my friends to drive around town, smoking cigarettes and haunting thrift stores. We spent our nights in dingy halls watching local punk bands thrash and scream on stage. But I never abandoned Shoshona. I spent my late afternoons with her, brushing her coat, cleaning her feet, absorbing the peace of her sturdy body and of the ranch. I lived a split life, as I found myself increasingly immersed in the punk scene, exposed to the bravado and violence, the brand of loyalty and respect that made me—the girlfriend of a key player—untouchable.

At seventeen, I didn't know how to deal with this sense of power. I didn't recognize the silliness or the danger in our feigning adulthood, in feigning toughness. During those years, the sense of vulnerability I had experienced simply existing in the world as a young girl seemed to evaporate. I moved freely. I spoke freely. If anyone insulted or disrespected me, an apology quickly followed once they realized whom I was dating. Holding such sway over adult men was completely foreign. Once, at a party, as I stood outside talking and drinking with my friends, a drunk man stumbled into me. His bleary red eyes made contact with mine and—hatefully—he spat out the word *slut*. I was stunned. Before I could react, one of David's friends intercepted and grabbed the guy by the shoulder. "You don't know who you're talking to," he told the man. "You need to apologize or you're never coming to one of these parties again." The drunk man was furious, but he mumbled an apology before stomping out of the yard.

Prior to dating David, I had never witnessed men apologize for calling a young woman a slut, for hissing disgusting words about her body, for acting as though she was less than. I now know that the vulnerability never disappeared; it was just misplaced. People were afraid of my boyfriend and his friends; I didn't realize that one day I would be, too. I didn't realize that my age and fear of returning to that sense of powerlessness experienced by young women made it easy for David to take advantage of me. He recognized my fear and used it to bully me like he bullied others.

I tried to get out of the relationship on multiple occasions over the next two years, but David reined me in until I finally managed to get big enough to make myself heard, to stay gone. This wasn't without a fight, though. As I stood in my friend Kassie's kitchen, clutching the phone, I took a deep breath and dialed his number. We hadn't spoken since he threatened to ignore me all weekend if I went to a friend's show instead of hanging out with him. I chose the show, having promised my friends I would go, having at least maintained that part of myself—the fiercely loyal part. It was Sunday evening, and I realized after a weekend of *not* thinking of David that I needed to get out.

My heart raced as I dialed his number. Kassie reached into her parents' liquor cabinet and pulled out a bottle of whiskey. She poured a shot and slid it toward me as the phone rang. I swallowed it quickly and continued to take shots through the entire conversation. The burn in my throat was a welcome distraction from what I had to do. Before long, Kassie motioned for me to look in the hallway mirror, and I saw that I had angry red hives spreading across my neck and chest. I don't remember much of the conversation; I don't really care to. But what remains with me is his wailing into the phone—a roar of emotion left unchecked. That night, after the hives had eventually vanished, Kassie and I went out with her brother and his friends, and I was sublimely relieved. More importantly, I felt unrestrained.

This didn't continue for long because David began calling the next morning. Pressing ignore with each call, I thought he would get the hint, but he would just call a few minutes later. He called again and again until I had to turn my phone off. In the days that followed, he'd show up at my house, smile to my mother, and ask to speak with me. She knew we were broken up, but I didn't explain the particulars because I was too embarrassed. I had been a strong-willed girl, who played football and hockey with the boys and wrote letters to the editor of the local newspaper. I had been raised to—had been willing to—stand up for myself, following my mother's fierce and loving example. My mother was proud of that, and I didn't want to disappoint her. I didn't want to hear myself articulate the words to admit that I had lost my way, that I had lost sight of the path she and my father had forged for me. Instead, I trudged up the stairs to my room, with David trailing close behind. It was the same each time. He would begin crying, begging me to take him back. With each word he spoke, I felt overwhelmingly suffocated, as though my body was so full of buried protest, of the buried words I wanted to scream at him and all of the buried rage I wanted to disinter, that I'd simply burst. Like a horse forced to submit, I stifled that anger.

Fortunately, during this time, I had been asked to house-sit periodically for the family that owned the ranch where I kept Shoshona; this provided me with the space and freedom I desperately needed to cope and regroup. David had been out with me only once to see Shoshona, and he couldn't recall the way down the narrow and nondescript country roads, with their rows and rows of peach orchards. The family's home was idyllic and peaceful. It was like a life I wanted and was trying on for myself. I would stand in front of the wide kitchen window and look out upon the pastures speckled with horses grazing and playing, their long necks arched gracefully, while the house cat weaved in and out of my legs. After my evening chores, I sat on the fence and watched Shoshona like I did when she lived at home with me, before my family moved to the suburbs. I watched her drift through the lush grass, dragging her feet, which had grown heavy with age, until the sun disappeared behind the mountains. I felt good and real and wonderfully alone.

At night, I turned my phone off, knowing that David would call or friends would want to go out; I sat on the family's outdated but comfortable couch with the cat on my lap and watched television or read, soaking up the quiet. In the spring and summer months, I sat on their porch swing, tipping it back and forth with my bare feet, and listened to the horses—the soft shifting, the breathy sighs escaping into the night air. Those nights alone reacquainted me with the girl I had lost touch with.

Although he continued to call incessantly—obsessively—David's surprise visits to my parents' house slowed as we put more distance between ourselves and the breakup, until he showed up one night while my parents were out of town. I had invited Blake, the guy I was dating, over to watch a movie, and as we sat on the couch, hand in hand, with a fire warming the room, the house phone rang. I didn't answer, but seconds later it rang again. The caller ID showed David's name; I answered, knowing if I didn't he would continue to call. He knew my parents were out of town and said, "I'm coming over." I told him he couldn't, that I didn't want him to come over, finally revealing that I had someone with me. "Tell him to leave, Ashley. I'm coming over, and he better not still be there." Having heard me arguing with David and telling him I would call the police if he showed up, Blake crept around the corner, concern drawn on his face. Blake was also a musician, and although he didn't play in the local punk scene, he knew about David and his friends. He knew their reputation.

Quietly, Blake and I made sure all of the doors were locked, the blinds drawn, and we found our places on the couch again, hoping David was bluffing. I tried to follow the plot of the movie but found myself straining to listen for cars outside. I knew Blake was doing the same. We started when the knock finally came— three swift raps—and I slowly made my way to the door. Through the dirty peephole, I saw David's face, blurred and slightly distorted. "You need to leave, David," I said through the door. It was met with frantic pounding. I said it louder, as Blake stood awkwardly in the center of the living room.

David remained outside for hours. Blake and I sat together in silence as David alternated between furiously slamming his fists against the door and crouching on the porch crying into his hands. Despite my fear and repeated threats to call the police, I somehow couldn't bring myself to actually do it. I was afraid of what would happen when his friends found out. I considered calling some of my own friends, but I didn't want to involve them, didn't want them to get hurt.

I hadn't planned on Blake staying the night with me, but there was no way he could leave the safety of my parents' house when David was outside in that manic rage. So he and I checked the locks again, turned off the lights, and crept up the stairs in the dark, afraid of cluing

David in to where we were in the house, knowing that his fit would only intensify if he figured out we were in bed together. As we lay in my bed, Blake pulled me close. I whispered my apologies for dragging him into this situation until we dozed off, so weary that the constant ringing of the doorbell no longer registered. A few hours later, we woke to a series of thuds against my window made by newspapers David had collected from my neighbors' homes in the early hours of the morning. As the sun leaked through my window, the morning finally grew silent. I heard a car door slam and knew that David was finished. He had exhausted himself after eight hours outside my parents' home and had set out for his own.

David's erratic behavior and intimidation continued until he found a new girlfriend. If I hadn't had Shoshona and the ranch during that time, it wouldn't have been so easy to return to the girl I was before him—before the bullying, stalking, and fear. I would have had to work harder to find myself again. In the years that followed, I grew steady once more. I rode and became strong. I remembered what it was like to know myself well. That isn't to say I didn't continue to struggle with asserting myself—I did. I still do. But Shoshona provided a space and an opportunity for me to cultivate a side of myself that is significant and definitive. I didn't realize it then the way I do now.

—

I've found that the way people talk about the love they have for their hobbies or for exercise is often similar to the way I talk about riding horses: there's the joy of movement, the stress release, the alone time. But there's an additional element to consider when discussing horseback riding, and in particular women and horses, and that is the horse herself. The horse propels this relationship toward something larger, more substantial. I now realize, after my work in Women's Studies as both a student and an instructor, and after years of delving into feminist theory, animal welfare, and horsemanship, that something is at work that is much greater than a simple hobby or affection for animals. This is an undeniably gendered relationship. Although the horse–human connection may have originated with men using horses for work and war, this continued and curious attraction women have to horses matters in that it has moved beyond utility and toward something more intimate. Horses represent what oftentimes women are made to feel we lack. They are powerful. They are strong. They symbolize freedom—the freedom that I desire so deeply, my skin crawls when I am denied it.

In some ways, we can also relate to them. In *Buck*, a documentary about the horse trainer Buck Brannaman, Brannaman describes why he became interested in a gentler version of horsemanship. He explains that after surviving intense abuse as a child, he understood what terror and fearing for your life felt like. Having experienced that trauma, he couldn't bring himself to incite it in another living being. Listening to him describing those feelings, I couldn't help but remember the day my mother and I brought Shoshona home—an image that is quick to reveal itself.

—

The white trailer stood parked in the driveway of the boarding facility where Shoshona had been kept by my aunt Erika. Shoshona had been afraid to enter the trailer for some time. I don't remember who was there or who played what part, but I recall the sharp crack of the whip behind Shoshona's hind feet. I know that she was being forced to choose between two fears, forced to submit to human dominance. In an effort to resist—to survive—Shoshona reared up, lifting herself into the air with her strong hind legs. For a second, she looked noble and unstoppable, like the horses in the movies. It was just a flash, though, because as she raised herself higher, the top of her head hit the roof of the trailer with a dramatic thud. As she stumbled back, a thin stream of blood trickled down her forehead, bright against her steely-gray coat.

In moments like this, I learned what dominance looked like, long before I would encounter it myself with David. I learned what submission looked like as well, as Shoshona grudgingly and fearfully stepped into the trailer, sweat creeping across her shoulders, which trembled slightly. I hurt for her the way children do before they are hardened by exposure to the world. And I now know that sympathizing with Shoshona wasn't so strange, nor is it strange that, as a woman, I still identify with horses. Along with our history of being aligned and affiliated with nature, of being subdued and conquered the way the natural world is subdued and conquered, there is the story of women gaining power through our communion with nature. This is a facet of our connection: It's about insulating ourselves from a sometimes hostile world; it's about considering the risk and understanding that the benefits outweigh the cost; it's about being a part of something much larger than ourselves as we participate in an extensive history—the history of the cowgirl, of the horse. When we ride, we hear the whispers of the cowgirl. It's about strength and steadiness, understanding and intimacy. It's about recognition. About identity.

For all the strength and power that horses represent, they are still prey animals—always fearful, always on guard. With so many women experiencing violence and trauma, it is unsurprising, then, that we may identify with our equine partners, who share not only in our recovery but also in our resilience. Through our work with horses, we learn ways of healing, of shaking off trauma, and ultimately of relating to the world without being victimized. For those of us who carry around a lingering terror that we can't quite shake after trauma, there is something invaluable in seeing that terror manifested in an animal who endures. There is something invaluable in drawing strength while identifying with the fear of the prey. In doing so, we share a recognition that holds deep and ancient roots.

In order for us to truly cultivate this type of mystical and astounding as well as fulfilling relationship, however, there needs to be a shift in the way we relate to our horses. Women have consistently reported feelings of unwavering love, friendship, support, and trust when asked about their horses. But would their horses report the same? We so easily fall into the habit of treating our horses as objects of our will and affection, and in the process, we dull their instincts and bury the many elemental lessons they can so readily teach us. Most often, we still interact with our horses using traditional forms of horsemanship that rely on submission and domination, no matter how benign these techniques may seem or how well-intentioned we may be. These are simply the prevalent approaches. We don't even realize what we are doing until we are exposed to more holistic forms of horsemanship that can lead to a fuller relationship—one that is rewarding for the horse, too.

Gentler approaches, sometimes called *natural horsemanship* for lack of a better term, are not new. However, they remain relatively marginalized because they require a slower approach to training, which often doesn't suit our needs. To practice these methods, we must watch the way horses communicate in their herds. I don't mean we should mirror it, as some trainers suggest. We must instead learn from the assertiveness and clarity in the horses' messages. We must slow down to watch how present they are capable of being as they graze in the pasture, and how hard they may focus on their fears. In studying them, we may learn when to stand strong and when to flee. There is an unseen risk with this level of attentiveness, though. Many times, we're forced to confront our past wrongs, and this can be a tough pill to swallow. But if we can muster the courage to grapple with our own sins, whether intentional or not, we all—especially horsewomen—can be better for it.

The world is at times harsh and heartbreaking for all of us, especially for women, given the societal, cultural, and political oppression we still face, so it is a shame that we have such abiding wisdom at our fingertips yet fail to become fully aware of it or use this wisdom. The connection is clearly there—we have decades of narratives to prove it. The potential is ripe. But it requires a broader shift in our thinking when it comes to our horses, a shift in how we form relationships with them. We must move from a relationship of exploitation—benign or otherwise—to one of true mutuality. And we can achieve this by genuinely valuing the integrity of the horse as an animal. By accepting equine instincts and desires wholeheartedly, we can work in harmony with those instincts.

We can revise the story of women and horses. 🐎

Lightning

SONORA'S HORSE, LIGHTNING, is sold off by her aunt as a punishment for her bad behavior. Sonora talks to Lightning, hugs him, kisses him on the muzzle, and loves him like I love my horse Shoshona. After the loss of her parents, Sonora is rootless—free to follow her wandering heart. Sneaking off into the night after a fight with her aunt, Sonora takes to the road in search of a traveling diving horse show that she saw an ad for, eventually finding her way to Atlantic City. As the movie *Wild Hearts Can't Be Broken* progresses, Sonora is blinded in an ill-fated diving accident, but in true Disney form, she perseveres and learns to dive without sight, continuing to do what she loves with her horse.

Sonora's diving horse looks just like Shoshona. He is stunning—tall and all muscle, with a silver coat, black mane and tail, and a small snip of pink on the tip of his muzzle. As a child, after watching the movie, I cut my blond hair into a chin-length bob and wore my breeches and tall riding boots every day that summer, just like Sonora, despite the suffocating Fresno, California, heat. Each evening, my boots, sticky with sweat and dirt, clung to my calves. I would plop myself onto the floor, legs sprawled in the air, while my mother pried them off me.

Sometimes, I would climb the fence separating Shoshona's pasture from our backyard and call her over. When her body lined up with the fence, I would reach out to grab a handful of her mane with one hand and feel for her sharp, bony withers with the other, before hopping from the fence onto her back—my own version of Sonora's mount onto her diving horse. I never wished I could dive Shoshona, though. That wasn't the point. What resonated with me most as I watched the film was that Sonora and her horse have a bond—glorified and romanticized in typical Hollywood fashion—that I wanted with Shoshona. Sonora loves and understands her horse, and he loves and understands Sonora. They are in sync. Together, they are strong and powerful. The orphan finds her home with that horse.

As a girl, I believed it when the characters in the movie say that the horses aren't ever forced to jump from such frightening heights, that they are trained and, more importantly, brave. Now, I flinch when watching the horses jump off ramps so high up in the air, crashing into the water below with a dramatic splash, especially as I know that the film is based on a true story. In the movie, the horse runs up the ramp eagerly as if it were what he wants, what he is meant to do. In a 1997 *New York Times* article by Bill Kent, Arnette French, the real-life Sonora's younger sister, maintained that the horses were well cared for.

In photographs and films of real diving horse shows, however, the horses are hesitant as they creep to the edge, easing their large bodies down low to the ramp before sliding forward and dropping off the platform. It is hardly the graceful soaring we see in the movie, and it certainly is not without fear. This is why diving horse acts declined in popularity after World War II as questions of animal cruelty continued to arise, before they eventually shut down for good in 1978.

I expected these feelings when I watched the film again as an adult. What I didn't expect was the way I knew how the story would play out—not because I remembered the plot, but because it simply seemed to be the kind of story that relies on the same narratives of girls growing up with horses that I'd been hearing for years, the stories I'd memorized so that they became more like gut feelings than clear articulations or vivid anecdotes. Most girl-and-horse movies, whether they are truth or fiction, play out in similar ways. I was embarrassed rewatching the movie, uncomfortable with the sentimentality and clichés played out on screen.

Set during the Great Depression, *Wild Hearts Can't Be Broken* begins with Sonora flipping through a magazine, lingering on a picture of a beautiful blond woman, her lips painted a vibrant red, advertising Atlantic City—the place "where all your dreams come true." Sonora rips the photograph out of the magazine before cutting her hair to match the woman's. Clearly, Sonora has a desire to be someone else, somewhere else. And why shouldn't she, an orphan living with her aunt, feel rootless? Why wouldn't she be enticed by the allure of escape? Although she is clearly aware of conventional beauty standards of the time, Sonora is not above climbing fences and getting dirty with Lightning, her huge horse with a broad chest, gleaming golden coat, and creamy mane and tail.

—

I used to beg my mother to let me sleep out in the pasture with Shoshona. Rightfully worried that my horse could trample me in the night, my mother refused. So I settled for devoting all of my free daylight hours to my big gray mare. I was practically raised on the back of a horse, but Shoshona was different from the others I had learned to ride on. Before my parents bought her for me, my aunt Erika rode Shoshona in various 4-H competitions. To my nine-year-old mind, being a show horse made Shoshona special, despite her obvious flaws. Notoriously stubborn, Shoshona was stoic and generally uninterested in humans. Still, I had the distinct sense that she cared for me in her willingness to humor me, the way she stood still while I stared into her amber eyes that seemed too deep to ever end, like images I had seen of space or the Grand Canyon. Sometimes, I climbed the huge pine tree in our backyard, inching toward the middle branch, which gave the best view of Shoshona's pasture. Leaning against the thick trunk, sticky with sap, one tanned leg dangling on each side of the outstretched branch, I watched Shoshona meander about with my brother's horse. It was peaceful being up there, watching over my mare.

As a child, anytime I was upset, usually at my parents or brother, I bolted out to her pasture, threw my arms around her thick neck, and buried my face in her shoulder. As I cried against her body, Shoshona twitched and sighed as she stood patiently before finally walking away, leaving my face streaked with dirt and tears. As I got older, I outgrew crying into her coat, but I didn't outgrow the need for her quiet presence as my desire for comfort increased with age. Standing near Shoshona, with all of her weight and heft, acted as a salve for heartache and sadness. Riding her, her body moving beneath me, her sides expanding and contracting with each breath, her head swaying as she walked, made me feel at home in a way that other things simply could not. As we galloped across the pasture, athletic and powerful, a rhythm between our bodies linked us in a way that defined my strength and physicality. Her body informed my own. This is the bliss of interspecies communication—wordless and passionate—that women find themselves enthralled by.

When I was sixteen, my parents bought a new house in the suburbs and relocated us from our isolated home tucked between rows of fruit orchards to be closer to town and to people. As we prepared to move, I had to find a job and a place to keep Shoshona, since selling her was never an option. I called various ranches, checked prices and facilities, and finally settled on one near our house because it was affordable. The new ranch was so close that I rode Shoshona over. Saddling her up at my childhood home for the last time, I ran my hand over her stomach before tightening the cinch, carefully lifting the bridle onto her head, and climbing on. We cut through the shadowy orchards to the canal running parallel to them and followed the water toward the ranch, toward her new home. Determined to keep and care for my gray mare, I started my first restaurant job as a hostess, cutting a check each month for Shoshona's board.

In my teen and early-adult years, homesickness struck often—a sense of yearning and unease that only the ranch and Shoshona could remedy. An anxiety disorder that was amplified by the usual teen angst had birthed in me a need for something settled and familiar—a feeling of home that Shoshona represented after our many years together. As we both grew older, Shoshona's health began to fail and so I couldn't ride her anymore, but simply standing in the pasture with her and the other horses, listening to them sighing and chewing, steadied me when I felt out of control. I stroked her neck and smelled her coat as I did so often as a child. Her smell remained the same through all those years, and it continued to comfort me.

—

Sneaking out through her window, Sonora hits the road in search of Dr. Carver's diving horse show after seeing an ad announcing his need for a new diving girl. Confident that she can do anything she puts her mind to, Sonora marches into Dr. Carver's tent. Dr. Carver, a surly and gruff man, refuses her, explaining that she isn't nearly strong or charismatic enough for the job. But the precocious girl refuses to leave. The current diving girl, Marie, is a star. She is glamorous in a prissy sort of way, clad in a white dress and spotless white gloves. In that moment in the tent, Dr. Carver manages to see something special in Sonora, as we knew he would, and offers her a job shoveling manure and caring for the horses.

Sonora has a wandering heart after the loss of her parents. Lacking roots, she's free to roam and follow her dreams. Many times, female characters who step out into the world alone, who speak their minds unabashedly, are knocked down. They are punished in some way or another. But not Sonora: She is rewarded for doing so. Her lovable stubbornness and confidence actually get her someplace. In a move that's not often seen outside of cowgirl narratives, the outspoken girl is celebrated.

—

As a teen, I played varsity tennis for my high school and acquired the nickname "The Wall," not for any unique skill or finesse but because I managed to get to everything. I was steady, my body reliable. And I was satisfied with that. I was proud of my sturdiness, my athletic thighs.

Over the summer break between my freshman and sophomore years, I woke up early each morning to ride Shoshona before the brutal heat set in, as I did every summer vacation. I grew leaner and my muscles tauter as the summer progressed. Upon my returning to school and tennis practice, my coach stared, evaluating my thinner body. "You've lost a lot of weight. You look great," he said, lingering on the last word. But he was missing the point. I was frustrated that my body was being measured in terms I didn't get to define. I wanted to be viewed as strong and tough, as someone who was capable and skilled. I flinched, sensing his eyes on me, seeing me all wrong.

I appreciate the sturdiness that comes with horseback riding and the work it involves with horses. When I clean stalls, I find value in the solitude and the ache of hard labor. Alone with the horses, I am free to let my mind wander as my muscles expand and contract with each stroke of the pitchfork. As I push and lift the wheelbarrow, the leaves of the eucalyptus trees tremble. Hawks screech overhead as brave crows chase them through the sky. I've heard people liken stall cleaning on Sunday mornings to a sort of church, and I can understand what they mean, not because I am a churchgoer, but because there is something about being quiet in the natural world, and performing a simple ritual, that makes me feel present and connected.

—

Al, Dr. Carver's gambling and womanizing son, arrives at the farm with a spooked but beautiful gray horse he won in a bet. To prove herself as a horsewoman worthy of becoming a diving girl, Sonora begins training the wild horse with Al's help. She names him Lightning, a tribute to her lost horse. Growing closer through their long training sessions with Lightning, Al and Sonora share their histories and dreams. They often lock eyes, lingering for a moment. Eventually, he gently and lovingly kisses her. That isn't as important as what comes next, though.

While Dr. Carver and Marie are practicing for the show, Sonora interrupts by proudly galloping Lightning through the gate, proving her potential. Impressed, Dr. Carver tells Sonora that he will train her as a diving girl if she can mount Lightning at the gallop. Sonora crashes to the ground on her first try, nearly breaking her nose. Dr. Carver pushes her to keep going. Fall after fall, Sonora continues to get up. Blood is smeared across her sleeve and her face. He asks her, "You going to cry?" To which she responds, "I never cry." Again and again, she tries and falls on her face. Finally, she thrusts herself onto Lightning's back. She glows in the triumph of her success.

—

I was about five when my parents bought Mittens, my little red and white Shetland pony, for $250. Our family having moved into a rental home with a bit of property, Mittens was our first foray into horse ownership. One day, while Erika was babysitting me, I raced around the pasture on Mittens, her short legs pumping away, her thick red mane flapping against her neck like streamers in the wind. I leaned forward like they do in the movies. Suddenly, Mittens planted her small hooves firmly in the ground, catapulting me over her head. I landed face-first, sliding through the dirt and crumbly bits of rock, bloodying my nose. Erika was worried I would cry and tell my parents, that they would blame her. To her surprise, however, I plucked the tiny fragments of rock from my cheek and got back on Mittens instead.

That's what you're supposed to do. Each time you are thrown off, you get back on. You certainly aren't supposed to cry. I learned that early on from my mother and Erika, who were both equestrians at varying points in their lives. And, of course, I learned it from the movies. Most of all, I learned it from my trainer, a hard woman unwilling to accept weakness. After graduating from Mittens, I briefly rode a horse named Misty. She was a lithe-looking Paint, with one steely-blue eye and one brown. But she was also unpredictable and mean, hardly appropriate for a girl my age who was just starting out.

At one of our weekly 4-H meetings, a group of us was riding around the arena while the trainer watched from the middle, calling out pointers and critiques. Unexpectedly, Misty took off, bucking high into the air, twisting wildly in an effort to loosen me from her back. As my small body bounced up and down in the saddle, I gripped the reins and the horn, somehow managing to stay on until Misty calmed down enough to keep all four hooves on the ground at the same time. I didn't want to cry, but I could feel the tightness building in my throat—a need for the sudden fear and adrenaline to find release.

Finally, the hot tears welled up in my eyes and trickled down my face as I was afraid they would. It was not the heaving, rib-rattling sort of crying. No fuss. As Misty and I continued around the arena, I avoided making eye contact along the fence, including with my mother, whom I could feel trying to catch my gaze to see if I wanted to get off. But I refused to look, embarrassed that I couldn't stop the tears from coming. I just kept my sight set straight ahead, over the tops of Misty's ears, as my bottom lip quivered. If the trainer saw the tears glistening on my cheeks, she didn't say anything. When she nodded as I rode by, I felt proud to have won her approval for staying on and riding it out.

I internalized these messages of cowgirl culture. You can be pretty but not too pretty to get dirty and shovel manure. Never be too pretty to take a fall. And you always get back up. Never cry. Keep it together. Meaning I could compete in the beauty pageants my mother liked to enter me in when I was a little girl—with all of the lace and frilly dresses, the glittering black buckle shoes, my blond hair curled and topped by a sparkly tiara the times that I won—but I couldn't let it interfere with my chores. And having a beauty pageant the next day didn't excuse me from being dragged out, in full camouflage, to hunt with my father. Country artists Brooks and Dunn, featuring perennial cowgirl Reba McEntire, promoted the same cowgirl values I'd been hearing about for years: "Cowgirls don't cry, ride, baby, ride." Cowgirls are stubborn. They have wandering hearts, as do the horses they break and ride. They are tough.

———

Because she lacks a connection with the horse, arrogant Marie is injured when she attempts to ride Lighting, so Sonora must fill in as the diving girl. This is her chance to be the star, her opportunity to make it to Atlantic City at last. Images of Sonora and Lightning are plastered all over town to advertise the show. However, after Lightning falls ill and is put on a brief hiatus, Sonora must jump Red Lips, who is spooked and agitated. Red Lips gallops up the ramp, but someone in the band slams his cymbals together, startling the horse, just as Red Lips and Sonora are about to leap from the platform. They twist through the air clearly all wrong. Sonora lands with her eyes wide open, and the flush of water causes hemorrhaging and blindness.

—

After I fell from Cody and fractured my vertebrae, part of me suspected it wouldn't have happened if I were riding Treasure. I thought that if I'd known Cody better, maybe I would have read his behavior and energy differently. Studying horsemanship in the years following my accident, I realized that those feelings weren't completely unreasonable. In my rehabilitation of Treasure, with the help of Shea, I started from the beginning, creating a strong foundation I could trust. Part of this involved building Treasure's mind and confidence by teaching him that he could release the stress that was buried deep in his mind and muscles after his many years on the racetrack. Both mind and body needed to be free from their constant state of tightness and worry. For him to be ridden safely, Treasure's mind had to be focused and present, his body free-moving and certain. This took a very long time, not like in the movies where change happens quickly. Certainly, Treasure and I had an initial connection, but it couldn't overcome his wildness and worry, and the lingering physical effects of strain and neglect. It wasn't so simple.

After five years of our work together, I now trust Treasure and know him well enough to read his signals. Even so, I still find myself worried and panicked when danger seems to arise, despite knowing that Treasure will see me through. I still carry the constant back pain that serves as a reminder that the human body is more easily harmed than I once believed.

On one of our early trips to work with horsemanship expert Harry Whitney at his property in Arizona, Treasure and I went out on a trail ride with the other participants. Warming up in the arena, Treasure moved smoothly and calmly. I felt as if he were truly with me. Then, as the other riders and I approached the gate opening to the rocky hills and the ocotillo bushes with their gangly branches, I felt Treasure's mind drift away from me. The connection from moments before had ruptured when his attention flew to the other horses and the unfamiliar terrain. Taking in my reins and putting a bend in his long neck as we walked a couple of tight circles seemed to draw him back. But this didn't last long.

As we started down the trail, Treasure spooked, launching himself sideways up a small incline. His body shifted beneath me and my muscles tightened, gripping the saddle. My heart fluttered in my chest and tears filled my eyes in response to the sudden and intense fear that I couldn't anticipate or intercept, rushing through me and vibrating tightly as it rolled through my body. From behind us, Harry called out, "Put a bend in him, Ashley. I wish it were as important to you as it is to him. It will save your life someday."

In that moment, fighting through my anxiety and through visions of my body crashing to the ground, I knew that Harry was right—that in order to ride safely, I needed my horse with me. Always. It's a constant process of communication and working by feel. I quickly put a bend in Treasure again, asking him a question, pulling his attention back to me, and he settled. I sighed as Treasure dropped his head and softened, but I was still troubled. We went on to climb the hills and walk across bridges, with his heavy hooves thudding as they hit the sun-bleached wood—things we'd never done before. I should have been elated at our accomplishments, yet I was still slightly unhinged as we made our way back to the barn—unable to shake the memory of my fall, as though it had become part of my being.

I thought I had known Cody, or at least horses like him, before the fall. Realizing that I was wrong, that I'd been too sure, too confident, made me afraid to ride him again. He wasn't like Shoshona, whose every reaction I knew by heart. Or Treasure, whose reactions I was learning through experience. At the same time, I knew I needed to get back on and work through the fear and apprehension chipping away at the image I had of myself as a horsewoman. I knew that I had to do what cowgirls are supposed to: I got back in the saddle.

—

Al steps in to assist Sonora with her daily tasks, but as we already know, Sonora is independent and stubborn. Relying on Al after her accident can't last long; it isn't in Sonora's nature. She must dive again. After convincing Al to help her by explaining that she and Lightning have a special connection that does not rely on sight, Sonora begins training again. The understanding between human and horse is the key. Her working with Al is unsuccessful, though. True to her heart, Sonora must go it alone.

She sneaks out into a dark and stormy night. Thunder rumbles through the barn, but Lightning isn't afraid. He is motionless as Sonora runs her fingers over his body, memorizing it—her thin fingers tracing the outlines of his muscles, pressing into his coat. On his back, Sonora sits tall. Satisfied. Proud. The movie ends with Sonora's voice saying, "I also found happiness with Al. We were married that fall and had a wonderful life together."

Lightning is glaringly absent.

—

In my 4-H group, the adults made a joke about the girls, saying they'd go one of two ways as they grew older. Either they'd remain devoted to their horses into adulthood, loving them above men and all else, or they'd discover boys and leave their ponies to grow lonesome in the pasture until each pony was sold to yet another young girl. I realized quickly that there was some truth in the jest. Boyfriends started appearing at the horse shows, gazing up at the girls sitting high on their horses. The older girls would sit casually in their saddles, holding the reins loosely between their fingers, laughing and flirting, while their horses yawned and dozed off in the sun.

One day, as the farrier crouched to file the jagged edges of Shoshona's hooves into smooth half-moons, he pointed out that as I grew older, I became more devoted to caring for my horse. And he was right. I diligently visited the ranch to be with Shoshona in her old age. I cleaned her hooves, lifting them carefully so she could maintain her balance on legs that had started to creak and ache. As I cleared the dirt and mud from her soles and brushed her coat, I noted the changes it had undergone over the years—from a glossy liver chestnut to a cloudy gray to a flecked white.

It wasn't that I hadn't discovered boys: I had, along with punk shows, drinking, and recreational drugs. Admittedly, I had one foot firmly placed in that world. But Shoshona kept me from drifting too far away, though at times I came close. Strangely, my experiences with cowgirl culture groomed me for the world of punk rock and circle pits. Toughness and swagger ran rampant in that scene. As I watched the band play from out in the crowd with my friends, the circle pit, a swirling mass of sweat and pulse, would rip past me. The crunch and screech of the music tore through the air that was thick with heat. Arms and legs flailed wildly in a crashing, chaotic whirl. The occasional glints of spikes and chains glittered. Beads of sweat rolled down my back, soaking my shirt. The frenetic need to move was infectious, and I jammed myself, slick and fierce, among the other bodies, each body working independently yet somehow being synchronized. I belonged to this unit. I moved with it. On the quiet car ride home, my body still pulsated and my ears hummed. After dropping my friends off at their houses, I turned the music up high, piercing the night, as I tried to feed and maintain the buzz.

While my friends were nursing hangovers the following morning, I dragged myself out of bed and drove to the ranch, where the sounds were softer and I was free in my solitude. The rich smell of alfalfa and grass helped shake off the fog of sleep and alcohol. Shoshona drew me back into my body as I rhythmically brushed the dirt from her coat, smoothing the fine hairs. I felt very strongly that the care I gave was my obligation, my pledge, the very least I could do after she shared her body with me for all those years and carried me safely into adulthood. I still do. For as long as Shoshona was alive, I would be homebound. 🐎

Nyxy and Cosmo

I IMAGINE NYXY, a stocky, barrel-chested Hanoverian mare, standing stoic and stony while the vet examines her. He is quick and efficient after decades of practice, and he can already smell the discharge. Just as Candace, who owns and manages the ranch where Nyxy is kept, has smelled it. Nyxy's owner, Hank, refuses to believe there's anything to cause concern. "I told those girls there was nothing wrong with this horse," he says to the vet. The vet stops him short, because there *is* something wrong. He can already tell that she's lost the baby.

The vet performs an ultrasound while Candace and Hank stand in silence, not daring to look at one another after weeks of tense disagreements over how to care for the horse. Although he's the owner, Hank rarely visits the ranch to care for Nyxy. He views her more as a vessel, paying little attention to her health and mental state beyond what is necessary to provide profitable offspring. He isn't unique in this. As the ranch owner, Candace bears witness to the mare's struggle and decline. She cannot simply ignore the mare the way Hank has, nor does she view the mare as mere matter.

The small, glowing figure of an unmoving foal fixed on the ultrasound screen confirms that the baby horse is dead inside of Nyxy and has, as suspected, begun to rot. From her uterus, the fetus has seeped into her system, spreading infection and shocking her body. To save her, the corpse must be removed. The vet and his assistant set to work, launching medicine and anesthesia through Nyxy's massive, bloated body, as the beeps of machinery float through the barn. They begin the grim work of removing the stillborn foal.

Exhausted, Nyxy remains motionless in the stall as medication flows within her, battling the infection. This sort of thing isn't new to the vet, but it still isn't easy. Finally, he rubs the patient mare's forehead, touched by her eager acceptance of care, and leaves her to rest overnight. He hopes that in the morning she will show signs of improvement. However, when he returns the following day, the receptionist is standing in front of the stall gate, shifting on her feet, fretting as she watches the mare struggle under the pain. The receptionist hears the vet's boots clicking down the cement walkway. She hears his fast and purposeful steps over the chirping of the barn swallows, and she turns to him, the lines in her face revealing what he already expected. Nyxy's system has been through too much. It is clear to the vet that she will not recover from the infection, so he euthanizes the depleted mare.

—

Sometimes in the morning, after riding Treasure or working my shift cleaning stalls at the ranch, I'd sneak into the feed barn and pocket a bright orange carrot. Breaking it into pieces, I'd offer it to Nyxy bit by bit. Nyxy's wariness of humans reminded me of Shoshona, spurring a tender affection and sympathy for her. After cleaning her stall and fluffing her cedar bedding so that it resembled a soft mattress, I would scratch Nyxy's neck, upper shoulder, and the very top of her back. As I worked my nails through her coat, the mare's eyes would droop and her lips gently quiver.

Every time I ran my fingernails over her, I looked for signs that she was ready to give birth. With her belly round and full, Nyxy began producing milk. Tiny drops hung off her teats. She grew increasingly restless in the days that followed. But then a stillness settled on her body, and she grew lethargic. The discharge came next. Candace told Hank that something was wrong, but he wouldn't listen. When the faint smell came, Candace called him again and insisted on taking Nyxy to the vet, explaining that it was her right as owner of the ranch to seek medical attention for a horse who was obviously distressed. She needed that extra leverage to get him to finally let her words through.

At the vet's office, Hank gleefully snapped pictures of Nyxy, still refusing to believe that the visit was anything more than an opportunity to prove Candace wrong. As an equestrian team coach and trainer, Hank was used to being right. After Nyxy's death, Candace and I stood in the shade of the barn and she said, "I'll never forgive myself, because I know if it had been a woman doing that I would have been more assertive. I would have gotten Nyxy help sooner." Candace released a dejected sigh that got lost in the sharp barks and rustling of the ranch dogs playing nearby. I knew her well enough to understand that what she said was true—that she was struggling with her inability to save Nyxy, with not having felt strong enough or horse-savvy enough to stand up to Hank despite several decades of experience.

—

On my thirteenth birthday, I sat near the fireplace surrounded by my family as I opened brightly wrapped presents from a neat pile. A pale pink envelope was nestled beneath the stack of boxes. Knowing it was there, and hoping it was what I'd been wanting, I prolonged the suspense, enjoying it. After opening my other gifts, crunching the discarded paper in my fist and tossing it into a trash bag, I held the card in my hand—the very last gift. Carefully, I slipped my fingernail under a raised edge on the corner, which was just barely curled up. Inside was a white piece of paper folded into a small square. As I unfolded the note, I saw dark ink peeking through and immediately recognized my mother's handwriting:

This gift certificate entitles to you one baby from Shoshona and Spatman. Love, Mom and Dad

I was thrilled, as most horse-crazy thirteen-year-old girls probably would have been—completely giddy at the thought of having not only a baby horse but one from my beloved Shoshona. For the first few years that I had her, my family lived next to a man named Jack who bred and raised beautiful Quarter Horses. People paid a stud fee and hauled their mares over to his ranch for his stallions to impregnate, but he was willing to waive his fee for us.

From the top of our haystack, I would admire each of the horses lined up in their stalls, their coats glistening in the afternoon sun. Most of all, I admired Spatman, who had a rich copper coat and graceful legs. I loved Shoshona so much that I wanted something from her, a lingering reminder of her long after she died. My 4-H leader told me that breeding a gray horse like Shoshona to a chestnut-colored horse like Spatman would result in a gray baby. She said the color would bounce back like a ball connected to a paddle. The baby was bound to look like her, I thought.

Jack often leaned over the fence separating our properties, his calloused hands resting on the faded and cracked wood, and watched me ride. In an attempt to show off, I galloped Shoshona in circles, paying attention to my posture and feet—back straight, heels down. Jack would nod or wave at me before walking back to his barn to finish chores. He told my mother that I was a quiet rider. I didn't understand exactly what that meant, although I hoped it had something to do with a sense of connection between Shoshona and myself, earned through our years together. If I raised her baby, I was sure I could achieve the ultimate connection: We would be intimate from the baby's birth and perfect in our closeness.

But things weren't what I had envisioned. Horse breeding is violent and harsh, and the way the two animals crashed together frightened me. Spatman's neighs were frantic and greedy as he transformed from elegant to ominous in a flash, pounding the dirt with his hooves, little puffs of dust rising around his legs. Shoshona, teeth bared, resisted at first, kicking out at him and spinning around on her powerful haunches. Afraid that his flailing front hooves would slice through her shoulder or connect with one of her legs, I winced from behind the fence. My heart raced and a sickness took hold of my stomach.

Veterinarian visits followed. My mother and I loaded Shoshona into the trailer and drove to our vet's ranch, going through our usual small talk on the way as I watched houses pass by through the window. When we arrived at the barn, I opened the heavy trailer doors and gave Shoshona's tail a gentle tug. She backed out, carefully placing her hooves on the ground as I reached up to grab the lead rope draped across her back. The vet approached and took the rope from my hands. He led Shoshona between two thick white bars, tying the rope to the end of one. While speaking with my mother, the vet wheeled his equipment over—a beige ultrasound machine with a small screen on top—and pulled a long plastic glove over his arm. I stood there pressing the sole of my boot against the weeds peeking up through the dirt, unsure of what was to come next or even how an ultrasound worked. As Shoshona stood between the metal bars, the vet wrapped her tail in a bandage and moved it to the side before putting his gloved arm inside her rectum. With what seemed like most of his arm inside her, he watched the screen, collecting images.

Regret seeped in, making my face hot and my arms shake. At the time, I couldn't formulate why I experienced such burning regret, but I knew if I vocalized what I had been feeling, I would have been told that I shouldn't be feeling it. I would have been told that there is nothing wrong with breeding horses. I would have been told that it happens in nature. Something in these justifications rang false. Now, I suspect it originated with the sense of powerlessness I thought Shoshona must have felt. As a young girl, I had already begun to understand what it meant to lose ownership of your body and the space around you, had tasted the shame that came with it. That I imposed my desires upon her body and forced it to bend to my will birthed within me a persistent and nagging guilt I've never been able to shake. At thirteen, I didn't understand the weight of my decision the way I do now.

Soon after, the vet told my mother that there was a problem. Shoshona was pregnant with twins. One fetus was absorbing all of the nutrients and growing larger and stronger, while the other remained stunted. I leaned against our avocado-green kitchen sink, nervously scraping my fingernails across the off-white grout, as my mother explained this to me. Listening to her speak, I found myself imagining a tiny horse figurine with miniature hooves, eyes shut, neck gracefully curved, floating within Shoshona's stomach. It would be risky to allow Shoshona to carry the twins to term and give birth, particularly since one or both of the babies would likely die. Or worse, Shoshona could. After relating all of this, my mother sighed, stared at me with her soft blue eyes, and said, "She's your horse: I support whatever decision you make." I didn't even have to consider it, though. I had put Shoshona through so much already that I refused to risk her life as well. I asked my mother to call the vet and tell him we would abort the smaller fetus, and then slipped off to my room to do homework.

Leading up to the birth, the vet and my aunt Erika prepared me for what to expect. Once, in the middle of the night, Erika arrived in her truck and drove me to her university's breeding facility. We were to watch a mare give birth. Walking down the empty halls of the barn felt eerie, as though we were disturbing the peaceful drowsiness that hung in the air. Some horses shifted lazily in their stalls, indifferent to what was happening in the very last one. There, a bay mare groaned as a bloodied and mucus-slicked body dropped to the ground.

—

We hardly slept the week leading up to Shoshona's due date. My mother and I took turns checking on her in the night. Crawling out of the warmth of my bed, I slipped on my shoes, not bothering to tie the laces. I left the lights off and tiptoed down the hallway through the living room and finally through the laundry room, trying to avoid waking the rest of the house. Out our backdoor, flashlight in hand, I broke through the still darkness with the glow of the light and the crunch of my footsteps. Half-asleep, I peered over the stall door, my eyes bleary and struggling to focus on Shoshona as she chewed contentedly on alfalfa, bits of it hanging from the sides of her velvety lips. On each of those quiet nights, guilt hung in the air between us. I whispered to her apologies for putting her through this; I told her not to be afraid, that I would be with her and keep her safe, even though deep down I knew I couldn't protect her from anything. I had already let her body be invaded; I had asked for it—begged for it, even. I wondered what my mother told Shoshona in the dark of night; perhaps she had some maternal advice for my big gray mare.

On one of my late-afternoon checks, I found Shoshona shifting uncomfortably in her stall. Racing into the house, I yelled to my mother, "I think she's having the baby!" My mother called Erika as I shot back outside. Shoshona's muscles tightened, and she groaned intermittently, occasionally pushing. Every few seconds, she released a thick sigh. Her ribs expanded and contracted under her sleek coat. Stroking her neck, I felt her body clench and release under my hand. A pair of diminutive hooves covered in shiny placenta began to appear. Gradually, a little more of the body grew visible: narrow, seemingly fragile legs; a nose rising smoothly up to a forehead; tiny ears that I wanted to cup in my hands just to feel their exquisite smallness. Reaching beneath the slippery mass, I guided the foal's body as Shoshona pushed. The dark of late evening gathered around us. Only vaguely aware of my mother and Erika peering into the stall, I was focused on Shoshona and the baby. Nothing else really existed in that moment, so intimate and magically unreal.

When the foal finally emerged, I cautiously lowered him to the ground. The pearl-colored sac didn't break, and I could see his face through the blood and mucus that shimmered under the barn lights. His eyes were closed, and his tongue poked out from between his lips. My mother handed me a knife as I knelt beside the foal. I wiped my hands on my jeans, creating dark smears across the thighs, and carefully cut through the thin layer of the birth sac. As I sliced, I was keenly aware of my hands, worried that I would shake or slip and nick the foal's delicate-looking face.

Shoshona gently investigated her baby, licking and nuzzling him until he opened his eyes and stirred. She tentatively poked at the sac that lay limp on the ground—a lingering ghost of wildness, her instinct guiding her to consume the evidence of a recent birth to protect her baby from predators. Stroking her neck, I watched as she nudged the baby to stand, encouraging him to move his wobbly legs. When he finally attempted to walk, his legs were uncooperative and unpredictable, as I knew they would be. A couple of times he got going, his lanky limbs each went in a different direction, and he lost control. I flinched as he crashed into Shoshona before collapsing onto the soft ground, legs tangled. Finally, he grew steadier and stood by his mother's side.

I called him Cosmo, even though I didn't particularly care for the name. My father thought it up, and
somehow it stuck. Shoshona was a good mother. She was
tolerant and loving, standing patiently while he nursed,
sucking hungrily. Each time, she remained still, relaxed
and calm, with her back foot cocked, as she nourished
Cosmo. When he was finished, they wandered through
the pasture together, Cosmo trailing her closely.

—

Weaning Cosmo from Shoshona was torture. As my
mother and I loaded him into the horse trailer to take
him to Jack's ranch for a few weeks, Shoshona whinnied
frantically. It broke my heart to hear her squeals of desperation and longing for her stolen baby. It hurt even more
to know that I was the one taking him away from her. But
everyone told me that it needed to be done. Shoshona
paced the fence for days searching for Cosmo, driven mad
by her grief. At the end of the first day, her coat was caked
with sweat and dirt, and there were ridges in the ground
where she pounded her feet.

This approach to weaning is common in traditional
horsemanship. In the wild, this process is much
quieter—a mere whisper. The mother, with the help of
the herd, does it when the time comes. I didn't know
that. I actually didn't know much of anything about
raising a baby horse. All of this was new to me, yet the

traditional horsemanship I'd grown up with had led my mother and me to believe that it would be a "project" I could complete by myself. Despite our best intentions, we couldn't have been more wrong. Training a horse to ride is a far more difficult and dangerous undertaking, something I was in no way prepared for. I still don't understand why any of us thought that I was. As Cosmo grew bigger and older and more imposing in stature, like his father Spatman, I realized that I couldn't handle such an enormous task, no matter how much I wanted to. And I certainly couldn't do it alone.

Between playing varsity tennis for my high school and having no experience saddle-training a colt, I was overwhelmed. My mother was just as inexperienced in this area as I was as a teenager with a colt on her hands, limited time, and no resources of her own to hire an outside trainer. The prevailing view was that you just "put miles on them." Each afternoon, I returned home from tennis practice, tired and sweaty, and stood in Cosmo's stall stroking his wide forehead, completely unsure of what to do with him as he continued to grow larger and larger. By contrast, my smallness became more glaring, more like a liability. I felt his unpredictability, his weight at the end of the lead rope, and knew of no way to create between us the type of connection I had imagined at the outset—the type of connection that had once seemed so simple.

Having reluctantly accepted my inability to follow through with what I had begged to start, I grappled with my options. Erika's fiancé, who was a cattle roper, had expressed interest in Cosmo, and I couldn't help but wonder if someone like him, someone bigger and stronger than I was, would be better suited to handle a green horse. At the time, for a horse like Cosmo, becoming a competitive roping horse, winning belt buckles and cash prizes, and working on a ranch seemed like a romantic path.

As the trailer pulled out of the driveway, carrying Cosmo away from his mother and from me, I wiped tears from my eyes and listened to Shoshona wail from her stall, calling out once again to her lost colt. For a long time, I didn't think much of selling Cosmo. Confident that I had made the best decision, I focused on making it up to Shoshona, knowing that I owed her something for her ordeal. Now, seven years after her death, I still believe that selling Cosmo was necessary under the circumstances, but accompanying that sureness is a haunting regret and a guilt that remain with me, and always will. I find myself wishing things had been different.

I know that by now, if Cosmo is still alive, he must look just like his mother. Shortly after Shoshona's death, Erika pulled me aside to talk in my parents' laundry room while the washing machine hummed. She placed a card in my hand, and then left me alone to open it. Within the envelope were pictures of Shoshona's early life. They showed Shoshona as a filly, her coat a shade of dark red, verging on a dusty burgundy. Flipping through the photographs, I watched Shoshona change from a liver chestnut color to roan and finally to a steely gray. Cosmo was born the same liver chestnut color that Shoshona was.

—

A few months ago, I asked Erika to contact her now ex-fiancé to see if he still had Cosmo. I wanted to tell him that if he ever planned to sell Cosmo, I would like to be the first to know, because I wanted the opportunity to buy him back. Her ex never replied to the emails. She is friends with him on Facebook, and his profile picture is of a brand on the hind end of a horse. The horse's coat is a dark red with flecks of white. Part of me wants to believe that it's Cosmo, that I've caught a glimpse of him. I want to believe that he's tangible so many years later. But then, as always, I enlarge the photo. It's of a horse with four white socks and a wide strip of white down his forehead. It's not Cosmo. Each time I do this, the disappointment feels new.

Candace says that all of the horses she has helped deliver have come back to her at some point. And I hope that this means something. In the wild, bonding is important. It establishes that an individual horse is a part of a herd. They belong to the band. Some horsemanship approaches advocate imprinting methods that mirror herd behaviors in hopes of making foals more submissive to humans—more easily trained. Beyond the politics and beliefs behind training philosophies, maybe we really can imprint ourselves upon these animals simply by being the first human to touch their little hooves, their downy coat. The first human to whisper in their ears. The first to love them. I know I'm aggrandizing those early moments with Cosmo, yet I can't resist toying with the idea that everything will work out because we are meant to be together, to transcend distance and circumstance. It makes the helplessness sting a little less.

The truth is there's a very good chance that I will never see Cosmo again, that he's been cycled through too many hands to ever track down, the way horses often are. As the years march on, Cosmo inches closer to death. And even if I do somehow manage to get him back, I know I won't like what I see. Although he'll look just like Shoshona and will make me feel for a few brief moments that I have her back, his mind will bear the marks of life as a roping horse, of a notoriously harsh style of horsemanship. Yet another reality I learned too late.

With Cosmo, I was still influenced by traditional horsemanship methods and didn't understand that by selling him as a roping horse, I was selling him into a life of domination, into a relationship between horse and rider that hinged upon submission and control. Selling him to just about anyone all but promised him that life. I know that now, so many years later, and this knowledge only exacerbates the guilt nestled within me. His body will bear the lasting aches from carrying the men who used him as an object, a tool for their work swinging heavy ropes over their heads, dragging writhing and fighting cattle, and twisting and turning to chase cows attempting escape. Worse, his mind will have been shut down. I've learned that he'll probably have retreated inside himself, a survival mechanism employed by horses when all of their options are taken away through traditional horsemanship training methods. I will have to face my guilt head-on.

———

Driving to campus one afternoon a few months after Nyxy's death, I saw Hank in the arena coaching the equestrian team through the glare of the sun on my windshield. For a moment, my heart started to beat faster, to thump angrily in my chest, and I thought I might hate him. I thought about the way he imposed his desire upon Nyxy, transforming her into simple matter, a vessel for his will. When Hank took her body, he took her life. I remembered the ways her body gave and suffered. In that moment, I couldn't help but also think of the ways Shoshona's did.

I may hate Hank's negligence and arrogance, but the truth is that I, too, am culpable. Although I didn't neglect Shoshona, we both asked our mares, fairly or unfairly, to give of themselves. Both of them did because they had no choice. And they gave for nothing. At times, I suspect that I am even worse than Hank. He never claimed to love Nyxy, never claimed that it was anything more than breeding for a profit. As they were leaving the vet's office, when there was still hope that Nyxy might recover, he even told Candace, "Once the vet cleans her up, I'll just breed her again."

Nyxy suffered because she was a commodity to Hank, while Shoshona was the victim of childish naivety, of good intentions gone awry. And Cosmo continues to suffer for the very same reasons. A desire born of love and ignorance continues to shape his existence, to harm his body and mind—a realization that was had far too late to do either of us any good. 🐎

Amber

DURING MY USUAL Sunday morning shift cleaning stalls at the ranch, I would stop raking and scooping to watch the horses scattered throughout the wide green pastures. Usually, they quietly grazed or napped with their large bodies sprawled out, basking in the sun as it warmed the earth. Other times, they pestered one another, with their teeth bared, twisting and chasing quickly and deftly. Each of the five sections of pasture was five acres in size, with horses assigned to a pasture based on age, sex, and disposition. The horses created their own little herds and families. The herd of mares in the pasture nearest to me was out at the far end, in a cluster, eating the last of that morning's breakfast. All but Amber, the old Palomino.

Stepping out of the stall I had been cleaning, I caught a glimpse of the mare standing by herself at the wide metal gate, swaying her head left and right, left and right. She seemed stuck in a trance, so far from the others. Sometimes, old horses get like that, though. They grow senile. Shoshona did. But Amber didn't seem uncomfortable or in pain, so I went back to work clearing away the small heaps of manure and pouring fresh cedar bedding for the horses to sleep on that night. As I pushed the wheelbarrow out of the stall, my thighs burning as I lifted it over a piece of wood used to keep water out, I glanced back to check on Amber. She was lying on the ground this time. Normally, I wouldn't be worried, but Amber had been having trouble getting back up, and she chose an unusual spot—the one muddy section that was shaded by the towering eucalyptus tree.

—

The first time I met Amber and her owner, Terri, I had been saddling Treasure at the hitching post. We introduced ourselves, and Terri asked if I wanted to go out on the short trail behind the ranch with her and Amber. We rode in between peach orchards, with abandoned fruit shriveling in the dry dirt, then through the vibrating orange trees that created a wall blocking the traffic we knew was near because of its hum. Over the rhythmic clicking of our horses' hooves as they hit the narrow farm road, Terri mentioned that Amber was twenty-eight. It was hard to believe that this horse, who managed to keep up with Treasure despite his having a good foot of height on her, was that old. Many horses die around that age, but Amber remained healthy. Her muscles, hefty and present, shifted beneath her gleaming coat. That was in the summertime, though. The cold and wet of the winter months can weigh heavy on old horses. Winter stiffens their bones, which creak out that song of the aging. Amber managed to hold out for a while, but soon enough winter made its home inside her, just like it had with Shoshona toward the end.

Still, Amber lying in the mud didn't necessarily mean something was wrong. Sitting on a hay bale in the barn, I watched Amber as she slept. The ranch was silent except for the sound of the wind passing through the branches of the trees and the high-pitched meow of the black-and-white barn cat doing a figure eight beneath my hand. Finally, the oatmeal-colored tips of Amber's ears perked up. She lifted her head and shot her front legs out from underneath her. When she heaved herself forward to get up, however, her back legs remained in place, curled up beside her. With her front legs still outstretched, Amber heaved again, slowly inching her hooves forward, digging into the mud. Again, her back legs remained motionless.

I called Terri, and as the phone rang I considered how to explain the situation to her, knowing that I should remain calm. Better to downplay Amber's condition than verge on the dramatic and scare her. I went to her voice-mail. "Hey Terri, this is Ashley. I'm out at the ranch, and Amber went down and can't get herself back up, so just give me call when you can so I know what to do. Thanks. Bye." I decided to look for Candace, the ranch owner, to see what she recommended. I walked over to where her house sat on the property, knocked on the door, and waited. No answer. Peeking around the corner, I saw that her little white car was not in its usual spot.

When I got back to Amber, she was turned around. Her back end had stayed in the center while her front half twisted in a circle like the hands of a clock. The poor old mare just kept trying and trying, but her body simply wouldn't cooperate. Finally, she collapsed, exhausted. She breathed heavily, and her deep brown eyes darted around, searching out the small sounds that her ears discerned. After all, horses are driven by the instinct to survive attacks by predators. No matter how far away they are from the freedom of roaming the open land with their herd, no matter how domesticated, their bodies still know the truth: If they are down, they are dead.

Candace called me as I watched Amber attempt yet again to get up, desperately reaching and digging with her legs, trying to secure a footing. Candace and Terri were at breakfast and would be at the ranch soon. As I waited for either of them to arrive, I sat on the fencepost watching Amber continue her rhythmic struggle. Front legs out, heave, collapse. Front legs out, heave, collapse. She breathed harder and looked more drained each time her head hit the ground. Her chest, once powerful and muscular, began pulsating from exhaustion and panic.

Her legs were smeared dark and ugly with mud, and her shimmery white mane was matted with dirt and twigs.

Terri got out of her car, holding a cup of coffee in her hand. She grabbed Amber's halter off the hook by the gate and slipped it over her mud-smeared nose.

"Will you help me?" she asked.

I walked through the gate and stood near Amber's face, noticing that her eyes had grown tired in that hour-long fight. Her heavy lids blinked slowly.

"My fiancé is coming to help," Terri said. "It took three of us to get her up the last time this happened. The vet gave her a shot of something to give her energy. Then, I pulled her head and he pushed her up from behind, while his assistant pushed from the side."

"So we're going to try to pull her up?" I asked, trying not to reveal my disapproval.

"Yes. If we can just get her up, she'll be okay. We got her up last time and she stayed up for three weeks."

Slowly, I realized that meant Amber's legs had been carrying the weight of her body for three weeks with no rest, no respite. It meant that she'd been missing out on the pleasure of sunning herself in the afternoon—those blissful moments with the rest of the herd. It meant that if we managed to get Amber back up, she would go another length of time without any real, meaningful rest. I suggested that Terri page the vet, secretly—

guiltily—hoping he would recommend euthanasia. I hoped he would convince Terri to end this struggle, but she insisted on trying to get Amber up first.

When Terri's fiancé joined us in the pasture, we discussed a plan. I would pull the lead rope attached to Amber's halter while he and Terri pushed from behind. We would wait for Amber to try to get herself up again and would then spring into action, building on her momentum. Terri started softly poking Amber in the ribs with her foot, prodding her to move; she told us that the vet had done this last time. But Amber stayed where she was, weary and burdened with age. Terri's fiancé went into the barn and emerged with a canister of sunflower seeds—Amber's favorite treat. Shaking the canister in hopes of luring her up again, Terri pleaded with Amber. The twinge of desperation in her voice was palpable. I recognized that desperation.

Amber glanced up for a moment, barely lifting her head off the ground, before she lowered it again with a thud. Terri poured some seeds into her hand and offered them to Amber, who weakly opened her velvety lips and caught some on her tongue.

As Amber chewed the seeds lethargically, Terri asked me, "How did you decide it was time to put your horse down?"

I knew I had to choose my words carefully. She was looking for guidance, for anything to make this whole difficult and murky situation easier.

"Well," I said, thinking hard about how to explain that I had chosen to do it before something like this happened, that finding Shoshona alone and scared in the wet and cold was my greatest fear as she started to age. "Shoshona had cancer and her legs were getting bad. She fell in the pasture and ended up with a pretty bad cut on her stomach. It healed fine, but I didn't want her to go through something like that again or fall in the pasture on a winter night and not be found until morning."

I thought back to the day I said goodbye to my beloved mare. As I waited for the vet to come and euthanize her after our thirteen years of companionship, I stroked her smooth gray coat, pressed my head against her cheek, and whispered my farewells as she breathed steadily, ears twitching at the sounds of the other horses in the pasture. I clipped a piece of her tail, a memento that was white with age. My mother and aunt Erika arrived before the vet to say their own goodbyes and to offer support, while I stood pitifully silent, afraid my voice would crack and give me away. The pressure in my eyes, throat, and jaw came in waves; I fought it off, unwilling to cry. But it became harder to keep the tears at bay when the vet's rumbling white pick-up truck inched up the drive. And it became impossible when he nonchalantly loaded the syringe and marched toward Shoshona with the needle poised. As much as I wanted to be there with my mare until her last breath, I couldn't stay without falling apart. Overwhelmed, I quickly handed Erika the lead rope and rushed out of the pasture before the vet reached Shoshona. Tears blurred my vision as I watched her smeared image shrink in the rearview mirror until, finally, it disappeared.

——

Terri stood quietly for a moment before saying, "It's just hard because they are so much a part of you."

And they are. Ask any horsewoman who has lost her longtime equine companion and she'll tell you the same thing. She may mention dreams of her first horse that still haunt her at night. Or she may mention cutting a bit of hair from her horse's thick tail for remembrance, as I did. The snip of Shoshona's tail sits on my desk, in an envelope containing pictures of her. I take it out every so often, hold it in my hand, and smell it. But it has lost that warm, earthy aroma I associate with Shoshona, and the bright white has taken on a yellow hue.

Shortly after Shoshona's death, a mutual friend, knowing I had a void to fill, introduced me to a woman who needed someone to ride one of her horses. This woman and I would spend the entire day riding across miles and miles of sprawling land, stopping midday to eat lunch and to share chunks of our apples with the horses as they rested for a bit. As we nibbled on sandwiches one day, she pointed to a grassy spot a few feet away and explained that it was where she took her horses when they were approaching death. She told me that when she knew the horse's time had come, she'd ride them to this remote place, ponying another horse to ride back on. She'd then shoot the aged companion, leaving the horse's body to decompose with the help of mountain lions and other animals. A few months later, she'd come back for the skull—a dull-white token.

At the time, I cringed at the morbidity of the act. I was struck by the strangeness of it and imagined rows of horse skulls peering down at her from the mantelpiece. I told my friends about this woman, laughing at the dramatic and unusual declaration of attachment to an animal. But now, seven years later, I understand. Having put some years between Shoshona's death and myself, I understand this need to have something that is so deeply a part of the horse, as they are so deeply a part of you. I understand the need to hold them again, no matter how dark it may seem.

As I write this, I have trouble imagining the shape of Shoshona's face, the wideness of her forehead, the place where, as a girl, I kissed the soft whorl in her coat. This inability to remember the shape of her face, the exact look of her, or the sway of her back inspires a vague fear and disappointment, because despite my reluctance to anthropomorphize or place too much importance on an animal's role in my life, Shoshona left an undeniable mark. Because she was in my life from when I was eight years old until I was twenty-three, Shoshona had been a fixture of my formative years. I grew up with her. She was my center.

As a girl, I admired Shoshona for her beauty and her strength. I remember wanting to be just like her because so often, I felt powerless in the world. I thought if only I could grow to be steady and fast and strong like Shoshona, then maybe I wouldn't be quite so susceptible to those feelings of helplessness. Or of shame. This was especially true on days like the one when I was in elementary school when a boy from my class trotted up to me on the playground, with a wide smile plastered across his face and a mischievous gleam in his eyes, and introduced me to my first namable bout of shame. He stopped about a foot away from me. We were face to face, and he said nothing before reaching for the hem of my shirt. Swiftly, he lifted it, exposing my round, childlike stomach. Then he kissed me. I shoved him away and told him not to do it again. As fast as he had lifted my shirt, he raised his hand and slapped me hard across the face. Even as a child, I knew that if I were bigger and stronger, he would never have been brave enough to do that.

I may not have been powerful out there on the playground, but I was while I was riding Shoshona. And caring for another living being, knowing that her life depended on me and that I, in a lot of ways, depended on her, taught me the weight of things. I know it's clichéd to say that having a horse taught me responsibility, but it did. It kept me honest. It anchored me. This became particularly important in my teen years, when feelings of shame and powerlessness continued to emerge—different versions of the very burn and sickness I experienced that day on the playground, but the same nonetheless. Shoshona carried me through them.

Shoshona didn't always act as a sort of equine savior and source of power in those days. She also represented a private part of me. If someone wanted to better understand who I really was—who I truly believed myself to be at the core, who I wanted to be—they could through Shoshona. My friends understood this. They didn't quite understand what it meant to care for and ride horses, but they knew it was a vital part of me. They knew that despite the parties and the punk shows, I was still a lone cowgirl at heart.

The first boy I loved came to the ranch with me once. I was house-sitting for Candace's parents, who also lived on the property, and he came to keep me company. We sat on the porch swing, with the stars above us and the moon casting its pale light over the pastures. The horses glided through the tall grass, grazing and sighing. Sipping beer, we talked late into the night. The following morning, we woke up early, while the air was still crisp, so I could ride Shoshona. As I rode around the arena, the boy drew on a large white notepad resting in his lap. Thin black lines converged to form the shape of Shoshona's body in motion. This boy saw that she mattered, that there was something special about her and the ranch that embodied who I was, who I had become through the years spent with my mare.

This recognizable sense of wonder, magic, and strength through my communion with Shoshona took on a greater magnitude when I entered college and discovered Women's Studies and feminist theory. I was left breathless when I read Carolyn Merchant's description of the "age-old association" between women and nature. Learning that the subjugation of women and that of nature had concurrent paths and persisting parallels caused my relationship with Shoshona to take on more meaning and nuance. Then there was Merchant's discussion of witches and nature:

> The view of nature associated with witchcraft beliefs was personal animism. The world of the witches was antihierarchical and everywhere infused with spirits. Every natural object, every animal, every tree contained a spirit whom the witch could summon, utilize, or commune with at will. (140)

Those words enthralled me. I'd never heard of communion with nature or with animals being described as something spiritual. Within a few sentences, we—me and Shoshona—were no longer simply a girl and her horse. Our relationship was richer and more compelling, as though we were engaging in an expansive, complicated history of women drawing power from nature. I was suddenly able to articulate what I had known in my gut to be true for all those years. Shoshona wasn't simply a hobby. Together, we were participating in something much larger than ourselves. For these reasons, I felt I owed her a pledge as she began to age—a promise to faithfully care for her *and* to know when it was time to let go. Too often, we humans fail to uphold that pledge, sending horses to slaughter when they grow impaired, inconvenient, or costly.

———

Before long, it looked as though Amber might try to get up again. Terri and her fiancé rushed behind her, clicking and clapping. Although I sympathized with Terri and could grasp how heartbreaking it was to see her horse in this state, I didn't feel right about pulling on Amber again. I didn't have it in me, and neither did Amber. Terri must have noticed that my attempts were half-hearted, because she ran up and grabbed the rope from my hands. She threw all of her weight against it, her face strained in a pained grimace, knowing that the stakes were high. Meanwhile, another horse from the pasture tentatively approached Amber. The mare sniffed at Amber before biting her hard on the rump, offering a little motivation from the herd. She, too, was acting on instinct.

When I left the ranch later that day, Terri was sitting on the ground beside Amber, and I gave her a weak wave as I drove past. I wondered if she was staying behind to take a few solitary moments with the mare, to say her goodbyes, to snip some hair from Amber's tail as a memento. I knew that I would find one of two things when I returned to the ranch the following morning. Either Amber would be dead and alone where she had broken down, or she would be with the others, resurrected by the power of love and desperation. Neither was particularly comforting to think about.

The bright blue tarp they had used to cover Amber's body must have blown off in the night, because it was crumpled next to her, with the ends flapping in the wind as I pulled up the drive, exposing her cream-colored face and the white star in the middle of her forehead. Her eyes were wide open and blank.

Treasure

WHEN SHOSHONA DIED after the cancer had set in and her legs had weakened and started to give way, I told myself I wouldn't get another horse. I couldn't imagine developing that bond, that relationship, with another equine companion. Shoshona was my horse love-match, and her death broke my heart, planting within me a grief I'd never experienced before despite the usual upsets of life—the loss of family members and friends. Yet at times, I tried to envision myself having another horse on some far-off day, to vaguely imagine what it might be like to learn a new personality and body, knowing they could never be like Shoshona's. That bond, I thought, simply couldn't happen with another horse. I certainly didn't expect to come across Treasure, my unanticipated project, a horse who would need me in ways that Shoshona never did.

At first an eerie sense of relief arrived alongside the sadness. On those icy nights, when the cold made my knees creak and pop and the rain pricked my skin, I didn't have to worry about Shoshona, about her aging bones in the brittle cold or her hooves softening from the wet earth after a heavy rain. I didn't have to imagine her in the dark weathering the storm, stoic and alone, her pale gray coat soaked and dripping, her head low and patient.

In time, however, the need to be in the saddle again began to nag at me. It was dull at first, like an itch. Faint. Abstract. It grew more intense as time went on—a deep-rooted longing. I replaced my devotion to her and to riding with working out. Riding was a source of strength, peace, and focus for me, and without Shoshona I was forced to seek them elsewhere. In the hours that I would have spent at the ranch, I went to the gym. Six—sometimes seven—days a week, I'd flee from the strain and bustle of daily life to focus on my body, on pushing it, on the ache of muscles and the sweat rolling down my skin, drenching my clothes. I worked out religiously, even on vacation and holidays; through the deaths of friends and loved ones, I moved my body. But no matter how much I wanted it, the gym wasn't the same as my time with Shoshona. The connection to the horse was crucial. It was the missing element in my search for peace.

———

Riding with Jennifer helped ease some of this longing. Taking to the trails early in the morning, with the chill of night still clinging to the air around us, tickling our skin and making the leaves and breeze feel crisp, we discussed everything from men to life goals. Our voices mingled with the steady creak of our saddles as our horses swayed rhythmically back and forth, moving together through the hills and thick brush. Those rides made us feel connected—to another person, to our horses, and to the world around us. They made us feel brave and powerful as we conquered the terrain—two women crossing creeks with our horses, ducking under low-hanging trees with their stinging branches, pushing our horses through the shadows of dense brush. And they served to emphasize just how much I missed having a horse of my own. We rode for a year together before I knew I was ready.

Before starting my search, I called Candace to tell her I was looking for another horse and asked if there was room on her property. There was, and she offered to keep an eye out for horses for sale. "What exactly are you looking for?" Candace asked. I paused, unsure of how to answer. Mostly, I carried around images of Shoshona and Cody in my head. "Oh, I'm thinking of a horse for trail and pleasure riding," I said, realizing I would need to finalize my criteria. After a lot of thought, I knew I wanted a calm, quiet horse—one who still had a lot of years left, but who had the settled demeanor that comes with experience after being exposed to trails and terrain. Beyond that, I knew I didn't want a horse who was white or gray: Shoshona was gray, and her color made her more susceptible to cancer.

With this in mind, I perused various Internet sites and inquired after the horses who seemed to fit. I spent hours scanning through pictures of horses and reading the sellers' descriptions of them: *Must see! Flashy! Does it all! Elegant!* One day, as I sat hunched over in my cubicle scrolling through ads for horses instead of working, I found myself lingering on one in particular. He wasn't what I was looking for at all, aside from his rather low price, but I read his profile out of curiosity. The listing said he was a retired racehorse, who was only off the track for a few months and was starting rehabilitation to enter the life of a "normal" horse.

Horse racing—what seems to be animal cruelty under the guise of entertainment—has always made me uneasy, so the idea of being able to rehabilitate a retired racehorse appealed to me. I had become a vegetarian a couple of years prior, having discovered animal ethics and the idea of speciesism, and I couldn't divorce that from my search for a new horse. But I'd always heard that off-the-track Thoroughbreds are notoriously unpredictable, flighty, and even dangerous in some situations because of their breed and the lifestyle they endure as racehorses—being confined in small spaces except to run, taught only to run, and manhandled by their caretakers. Thoroughbreds have been crafted to be the perfect athletes. Carefully guided selective breeding has created a horse who is fragile and simultaneously pure power and speed. They are truly exceptional animals, but they are often too much horse for the average rider, and I wasn't sure if after my hiatus from riding, I could handle so much energy and drive.

I found myself returning to his profile nonetheless. His name was Treasure. He was tall and lean, muscles defined under his dark brown—almost black—coat. His elegant appearance was the complete opposite of Shoshona's, with her light gray coat and stocky build. Perhaps that is why I kept going back. Perhaps I knew it would be easier to move on with a horse so entirely unlike Shoshona. The seller described him as gentle and very people-oriented, but I was skeptical considering his racing past.

I consulted Erika to see what she thought, and she suggested that I go see him, pointing out that I might as well ride as many horses as possible before making a decision. The next day, I contacted the seller and made arrangements to meet Treasure. On the phone, the woman seemed nice, but there was something about her that didn't quite add up, making me question her motives. As I took notes at my desk, careful to shield them from co-workers passing by, she explained that she was selling a few off-the-track horses whom she was rehabilitating for an owner in Idaho. I got the sense she was involved for the profit rather than to give these horses an alternative to neglect in pasture, euthanasia, or a trip to the slaughterhouse, but I reminded myself that many in the horse industry are in it for profit.

And that isn't so unusual. By simply making it that far, to that woman Treasure had fared better than many off-the-track Thoroughbreds who have landed at auction and been sold for meat. Even famous racehorses have found themselves on their way to slaughter after every dime has been squeezed from them. Although we do not eat horses in the U.S., they are considered livestock, and like their counterparts—cows, chickens, and pigs—they experience unspeakable cruelty behind closed doors at the slaughter plant. In her heartbreaking essay "Dark Horse," Lisa Couturier explores in painstaking detail what happens when camp ponies, retired show horses, and off-the-track Thoroughbreds end up at the kill auction.

I arranged to visit the ranch where Treasure was kept. Pulling in, I scanned the pastures for a black horse like the one in the pictures but didn't see him, just reds and browns with their heads nestled in patches of grass. I parked and wandered toward the stalls, where a short blond woman stood. After we shook hands, she left to get Treasure. I watched as she walked toward a large, uncovered paddock. There stood a horse who looked nothing like the picture aside from his height. As she led him toward the hitching post, the unhealthy narrowness of his body became fully and depressingly evident. Rubbing his neck, I felt the coarse, sun-bleached hair poking through my fingers. The way he towered over me was intimidating, yet he was painfully thin, as thin

as an older horse approaching death might be, not a sev-
en-year-old who had barely finished growing. Each rib
was visible beneath his coat, leading toward protruding
hip bones—I ran my fingers over them and felt them rise
and dip through his pitiful coat. His hooves, too, were
clearly neglected and overgrown, with each one cracked
and chipped.

The woman must have caught me evaluating the signs
of inattention and lack of care visible on Treasure's body
and seen the disgust I tried to hide. She spoke up quickly.
"He's really underweight," she said. "I've actually put a
hundred pounds on him since he's been with me. He just
got his teeth done so that should help put some more on.
Do you want to watch me lunge him?" she asked, quickly
changing the subject. Clipping a lead rope to his halter,
she led Treasure to the arena, where she made him move
circles around her, driving him with a long black whip.
Treasure's movements were graceful, despite the look of
him. His slender legs, the only elegant-looking part of
his body, swung out, free and fluid. After he had circled
her a few times, she brought him in and asked if I wanted
to ride him. He seemed settled enough, so I saddled him
up, doing my best to ignore the guilt I felt for putting my
heavy trail saddle on his bony back.

Riding Treasure in small circles, I found that his
walk was smooth and quick; my body was moving with
each of his motions, swaying back and forth with him,
synching up. And that movement, achieved so quickly

between us, was akin to what I had had with Shoshona. He was clearly unfinished and needed a lot of work, which was something I hadn't planned on doing with my next horse, particularly since I was preparing to enter graduate school. However, despite these glaring deviations from my thoughtful criteria, I was sure we were a match. More importantly, I could see blatantly written across his body his need for someone to nurture him. Someone to save him.

As I brushed Treasure down after our ride, I was reminded again of how much he was lacking. He watched me as I ran the brush across his neck, and I saw that his eyes were sensitive and deep. And they were strange, not like Shoshona's—amber and strong. Treasure's were needy and dark and sad-looking. Leading him back to his stall, I already felt a slight pang of regret that I was leaving him; I already felt too much. I decided I should come out again with Erika, who could be objective. I can't really explain why I was so willing to veer from the attributes I had thought I wanted, but I was drawn to him, to his need. I knew I could help him—bring him back. As I was anticipating the seemingly inevitable breakup with my boyfriend Jake, I suspect that I needed Treasure, too. Perhaps I yearned for something to pour myself into, for a way to savor the aloneness around the bend.

As I waited for Treasure to be delivered to the ranch, the place where Shoshona lived out her last years, I ambled around, making sure to avoid looking at her old pasture, knowing I couldn't do so forever. Everything appeared the same. The eucalyptus trees still rose high into the air; the delicate silver dollar leaves still dangled. The pasture remained green and lush. Soon, Candace came to join me, and we made small talk until a truck and trailer peeked around the corner and crept up the drive.

The woman popped out, barely saying a word to us as she opened the doors to the trailer and entered. As she led him out, Treasure's eyes were filled with panic and his muscles tensed. For the first time, Treasure actually looked like a racehorse and I immediately thought, *I just bit off more than I can chew. I can't handle this horse.* Candace looked concerned, her brows furrowed, lines leaking across her forehead. I could tell she thought that I had made a bad decision, that Treasure was unsafe and a mess. As the woman handed me his lead rope, I was aware of his physical power in a way that I hadn't been in my life with horses. Treasure followed me, but there was a sharp distance between us. As I stood small beside him, I sensed that his mind was fixed elsewhere. His weight on the end of that lead was entirely separate from me, charging the space between us, making me nervous.

I managed to get him into a stall, where I gave him some food and time to assess his new surroundings. Pacing the bars of the stall, only stopping occasionally to pull a bite of hay from the feeder, Treasure started to sweat and tremble. He pawed the ground, etching rough scratches and grooves into the dirt. The whites of his eyes glowed harshly against his dark coat. When I left him that afternoon, he was still pacing restlessly, hours after his arrival.

Alone in the silence of my room that night, I was sick with regret and worry that Treasure wasn't the horse I thought he was, that I should have just stuck with my criteria. After all, they were my criteria for a reason, and I shouldn't have abandoned them to save an animal who I thought needed me. I fretted, thinking that perhaps this was an example of what my counselor and I were trying to work through—my readiness to ignore the boundaries I set for myself in order to help someone else, my readiness to give too much of myself. But in the rush of second-guessing, I told myself that I was just letting Candace's reaction undermine what I knew to be true. I had been on this horse, and he felt right. Treasure was simply nervous arriving at a new place, expecting to be raced. I reminded myself that I needed to trust my instincts—yet another thing my counselor and I were working on.

Eventually, my fears were dispelled. Candace spent some time with Treasure and realized what a kind horse he was—how sweet and gentle he was—although there was no denying that he needed a lot, even more than I had anticipated when buying him. Suddenly, I was looking at a money pit. Although I could work off the cost of board by cleaning stalls, everything else related to horse husbandry was quite costly, and growing more so. Horses are exceedingly easy to acquire, with so many being simply given away or sold for the price of their flesh, thus making them vulnerable to kill buyers, when owners can no longer afford their care.

Shoshona was an easy keeper, so everything was new to me as an adult approaching Treasure's care on her own, without the help of her mother. Fortunately, Candace offered sage guidance. Most pressing was Treasure's inability to eat properly. The woman I bought him from had been either lying or mistaken when she said his teeth had been taken care of, because grain poured from the sides of his mouth with each bite and bits of hay were always left over despite his desperate hunger and voracious attempts at eating. Without having his teeth fixed, he would never put on the weight he needed. Candace had a dentist who worked on many of the horses at the ranch, and so we made an all-day appointment.

When I arrived at the ranch that morning, the dentist had just finished tending to another horse. I held Treasure's lead rope as she readied a syringe with a sedative. Soon, the sedative set in, weighing his body down, softening it. Still awake but barely, Treasure teetered in his stall, relaxed and drowsy. The dentist approached with a metal contraption connected to thick leather straps that she fixed to his head. It held Treasure's mouth open so she could work freely. The contraption looked grotesque hanging on Treasure's face, his mouth opened wide enough for her hand to fit inside, bared teeth resting on the metal pieces. It seemed like something from a horror movie. Reaching into his mouth with her manicured nails painted a pale and glittery pink, the dentist felt his teeth, searching for the cracked, jagged pieces, the uneven spots. She suggested that I reach into his mouth to touch them myself. The idea appalled me because it seemed so unnecessary, so invasive, and yet I did it, compelled to understand what had to be done. Moving my hand past his lips, past the bottom one with the identification number tattooed on the inside—something given to all young racehorses— my skin brushed across his moist, thick tongue before finding the teeth. They were sharp and jagged as I ran my fingers across the top of them, noting the places where they lacked, the places that rubbed against the tender flesh on the inside of his cheeks.

The dentist instructed me to place one hand under his face and one hand near his ears to hold his head up as it grew heavy with the weight of drowsiness. While I held Treasure's large face, the dentist grabbed something from her case hanging from the stall gate—a small electric tool with a round metal blade. It spun quickly, making a low squealing noise. Panic rose in my chest as she moved closer to his mouth. I wanted to stop the whole operation, but knew that Treasure needed it to eat properly, to put on the weight he so clearly lacked.

As the dentist set to work on his front teeth, Treasure jerked his head up suddenly, lifting me to my tiptoes along with it. Seeing me struggle to hold his head and keep my balance, Candace swiftly moved to the other side to hold him as well. After we lowered his head, the dentist set to work again, filing his teeth. A fan blowing in the corner caught the bits of dust and shot them into my face. As I turned my face away from flying dust and the brutality of blade against teeth, I looked up at Treasure's eye and saw it roll back, exposing pink blood vessels, before rolling forward again.

Once the shaving was completed, the dentist needed to file the rough edges. This seemed so much more civilized than the blade, but the sound of metal grating against teeth made my skin crawl. The whole ordeal was more traumatizing for me than for Treasure, who'd been mostly motionless, aside from a few moments when he jerked his head against the strangeness of hand and tools in his mouth. But he couldn't see what was happening to him. He only felt the slight pressure on his teeth and heard the bizarre noises near his face. Seeing everything, especially the tools—seeing the invasion of his teeth in the name of what was good for him—made me feel responsible and fully aware in a way that inspired guilt for the things I had to do to help him recover.

When the dentist was finished, she took the contraption off Treasure's face, and Candace and I released his head. I hadn't realized how sore my arms were from holding his head up until I lowered them, stiff and achy, to my sides. Treasure was still woozy as the dentist packed up; he rested his head gently on my chest while I rubbed his ears, admiring their graceful curves, more deer-like than horse-like. That moment was peaceful and tender as he rested and I inhaled his earthy, animal smell, the fine hairs on his forehead touching my own, and appreciated the intimate moment of stillness shared with my new horse. And I remembered moments like this I had shared with Shoshona, my arms wrapped around her neck, my nose pressed into her coat. Treasure's eyelids lowered in slow blinks as the haze started lifting. As I stroked his ears and face, I thought about what had just happened. I felt disgusted at the process and simultaneously an odd sense of community with Candace and the dentist, because we were there. We did it ourselves, as women, displaying a sense of independence I was proud of.

The first step in rehabilitating Treasure was completed, and over the following weeks Candace and I discussed the many other problems that needed to be addressed. Desperate, I used some of my student loan money to enlist the help of a chiropractor and a trainer in the slow and difficult rehabilitation process. At first, I felt silly having a chiropractor work on my horse, because at the time, I still had not seen one for my own back problems. However, racehorses often sustain injuries and strains causing chronic pain and stress on their bodies, so I wanted to address his first.

When the chiropractor arrived, I was nervous. I wasn't sure how Treasure would react to being pushed and prodded; I knew that if he wanted to overpower me, he could. The chiropractor ran her hands along his body, and I saw him flinch and quiver as she located the spots where he required work, particularly on his neck. As she made her subtle adjustments, she spoke to me over her shoulder. "His neck is upside down, which means it looks like an upright letter U when it should look like an upside-down U," she said. Stopping, she faced me and used her hands to demonstrate.

This painful curvature of his neck was directly caused by the constant pull of jockeys during races and by the way horses brace their bodies against the bit until it becomes a chronic condition. Treasure stood patiently as the chiropractor finished making her adjustments and showed me some exercises to do with him to reshape his neck and eliminate some of the pain. At the end of her visit, she handed me a diagram of a horse, on which she had drawn angry red-ink scribbles indicating where his problem spots were. Scribbles covered the entire neck and back of the paper horse.

Treasure's one-year anniversary off the track came shortly after the chiropractor's visit. His final race had been at the annual Fresno Fair, and as the fair rolled in, I considered going. I knew I would be a hypocrite, viewing a sport I openly criticized, especially after seeing firsthand the damage (and not even the worst of it), but I was undeniably curious. I wanted to see for myself what Treasure had experienced, how the damage had been inflicted. I wanted to observe what it looked like to the person being entertained by it, paying for it, endorsing it.

Before the horses were lined up, men marched them by the crowd for the gamblers to size up. The horses—sweaty, glistening, wide-eyed, petite jockeys perched atop their backs—pranced nervously as they were each led by a rider on another horse. Reins were drawn short, clutched tight in the jockeys' hands, taut across the arched necks of the horses, who were braced against the weight of the jockeys pulling on their mouths. Every horse had a white string drawn through their mouth and under their chin, effectively tying their tongue down. I wondered why it was important that the horses couldn't move their tongues during a race. I later learned that racehorses' tongues are tied down so they don't swallow their own tongues as they run.

The race started, and soon the horses sped by in a vibrating cluster of muscle, sweat, and mud. After the first group barreled through their race, my friend and I stuck around for the one that followed. We walked to the viewing area, where the horses were taken for a closer look before bets were placed. Handlers led them around in circles as people gazed upon their bodies, evaluating and speculating upon their potential for speed. A couple of horses looked like Treasure—dark bays with long thin legs and thoughtful eyes. Almost every horse had a thick gold chain strung from the top of their halter across their nose and connected to the lead rope their handler held. This granted the handlers more control over the amped-up animals.

Most of the handlers kept a steady pressure against their horses' noses, but there was one who made a succession of short jerks. As the chain smashed into cartilage, the handler hurt the horse into submission, or at least enough to get him around the circle. The only horse who didn't have a chain strung across his nose had one strung through his mouth, easily smashing against his teeth, tongue, and the sides of his lips. I couldn't help but think of Treasure's teeth, jagged and cracked, neglected and uncared for. And as I thought about his teeth, my mind wandered up his face to the bridge of his nose, where the chains had once been. I recognized the raised cartilage, permanently swollen from past trauma.

—

When I was a child, I often used a chain when leading Shoshona. My childhood trainer, Carol, told me to jerk on it when she wasn't paying attention or when she pulled away from me. If Shoshona wasn't responding properly as I rode her, Carol used to order me to get off. She'd march over and rip the smooth leather reins from my hands and pull on them hard, causing the bit to crash against Shoshona's tongue and mouth. My stomach churned, bubbling toward my throat and making it feel acidic and harsh whenever I stood by and watched these things happen to Shoshona, whom I loved so much. But I was just a child. I didn't have the guts or the voice to speak up for my big gray mare.

———

I enlisted the help of Shea, Treasure's craniosacral therapist who was also a gifted horsemanship trainer. She echoed the diagnosis of the chiropractor and pointed out a number of other physical ailments, including ulcers, that Treasure suffered as a result of racing. Not only was his neck upside down, but he'd also experienced cartilage damage across the bridge of his nose (I once again thought of that day at the races). Although he was seemingly calm, there were a few subtle signs that internally he was not as settled as he appeared, particularly with regard to his mouth and stomach. Treasure's mouth was in constant motion as he was ridden. His tongue would rapidly swish side to side, and his mouth would foam.

There's a widely held belief in the horse world, particularly among dressage riders, that foam means relaxation; although it can, that's not always the case. In dressage, horses strapped down with the most drastic of bridles will drip white foam from their mouths, filled to the brim with worry. For us, the goal was to get Treasure to understand that the weight of reins no longer meant racing or stress. The aim was to get his mind settled and his head to a good place—a safe place—and make him softer when I lifted a rein instead of bracing against it as he would with a jockey. Shea's approach was not about "attitude adjustments" and yanking on a horse's face until he submitted, but a holistic emphasis on communication with the horse's body and thought.

A friend recommended that I watch the movie *Secretariat* for its beautiful shots of racing and the way the famous racehorse is represented as if he were driven by a desire to run that was born in his heart, as if it were innate. I could see what my friend meant. The characters repeat this sentiment over and over: Secretariat *wants* to run. The horse is made out to be a hero. Yet for all the scenes featuring the shimmering red horse, nicknamed "Big Red," I'm not sure we ever really *see* him. Instead, we see our projections of him. I concede that horses can and do enjoy running for the sake of it—I've seen it myself when Treasure takes his evening loops around the pasture, his head swaying side to side, blissful in the sheer joy of movement. And Secretariat is a magnificent horse and athlete. But I know, too, that racing isn't at all the same as running freely or out of the instinct to roam and cover miles.

I looked up Treasure's racing record online—his losses and wins, profits, and where he raced. A website even showed videos. I hesitated for a moment before I pulled out my credit card to buy the right to watch him race, knowing I wouldn't like seeing the jockey pulling hard on his face and neck, whipping him, pushing him to go faster and faster. However, just as with the Fresno Fair, I was also strangely compelled to watch it for myself, to know where Treasure came from—the life he had had prior to me. I already knew from the woman who sold him that Treasure wasn't a particularly successful race-horse, and from his record, I learned that he had earned his owners only a little over $10,000 whereas his sire had earned close to $600,000. I also discovered that before his arrival in California, Treasure had lived in Kentucky and raced in Idaho.

Watching Treasure blaze around the track, his tail floating behind him, legs pumping furiously, I couldn't help but try—in vain—to make out the curve of his neck, the white spot above his left hind foot, the point of his ears. I strained to recognize my horse, to see him as more than part of the mass. I couldn't help but search for the source of the brace in his body that I had to work so hard to release.

Most people when they learn I have a retired race-horse ask if he is fast. To avoid a lengthy answer, I usually just say that he is. I do this so I don't have to explain that the brace in his body, a result of stress and his training for the track, created in Treasure a stickiness, a reluctance to move. At first, I could hardly get him to trot, let alone canter or gallop, without the stress building, without his mouth moving furiously. If I hadn't learned better horsemanship approaches, hadn't learned to recognize small signs of stress that are easy to ignore, I would have overlooked his anxiety and forced him into movement.

Instead, with the guidance of Shea and Harry, I spent nearly a year working to get him to leap into a canter cleanly. The first time he did, Shea said, "I wish we could just run him and let him get all this brace out." She told me about her own horse, one who carries his stress in a way similar to Treasure—deep in the muscles, tight across the shoulders and chest. One day, while riding in a broad and open space, she simply let her horse gallop. He needed to just *go* to see that it could turn out all right. Treasure did, too. So, we made do. Shea stood in the center of the arena with a lunge whip and told me to loosen my rein, to hold on and guide him, but mostly to just let him run.

As he walked, then trotted, and then—with the help of Shea on the ground—cantered, Treasure's muscles felt tight beneath me. As we turned the corner and straightened out, he surged forward, and I resisted my initial urge to slow him. I held on as he picked up speed. Holding onto the pommel with one hand, I reached forward to rub his neck with the other. His breathing was stunted at first. Before long, though, it steadied. Looking down at his shoulder, I saw it relax and soften; I felt his body lengthen and release. I even caught a glimpse of him licking and chewing, a sign of contentedness and relief in horses.

When I was learning to ride and interact with horses, much of my training came from the opposite end of the spectrum. It relied on force. Riders around me often used tie-downs to trap the horses' heads in place, whips to move them forward, and heavier-than-necessary bits in the horses' mouths to control them, which achieved accelerated results. These methods don't require time like my work with Treasure did. They don't require that the horses feel okay about anything happening to their bodies, only that they submit. In my childhood self's eyes, these methods didn't seem overtly cruel, mostly because they were all I knew, but neither did they sit right with me.

Now, as an ecofeminist who has the opportunity to develop this other approach to horsemanship, I have embraced it because it disrupts the traditional approaches that are patriarchal in attitude. Through a patriarchal lens, says Merchant, "[d]isorderly woman, like chaotic nature"—wild woman as well as wild horse—"needed to be controlled" (127). I have grown up hearing women and horses talked about in much the same way, even down to the commonly held belief that mares are "bitchy." I've had more than my fair share of trainers essentially tell me that a horse needed to be put in their place. By contrast, Harry's tenderness toward the horse is refreshing. My enthusiasm for the approach doesn't mean I don't make mistakes constantly. And Treasure forgives me because that is what horses do, time after time, whether we deserve it or not.

Our work has made Treasure healthy and strong. His ribs no longer glare harshly from around his belly, his coat shimmers in the sunlight, and those sad eyes are now bright and content. With me, he is finally free to be a horse, something he's been denied during his racing career. Yet, he also requires guidance and teaching, as well as care that at times leaves me uneasy, which is where I can fall down the philosophical rabbit hole of parsing degrees of harm. This care, including his dentist's appointments, is necessary, and I remind myself that I'd never do anything beyond what is needed for him to thrive. Still, I'm not entirely sure where to best strike the balance between maintaining an animal's sense of autonomy and caring for them in a place that does not provide much space for so many animals who are independent of humans. Nor am I completely sure where Treasure and I fit within humans' barbaric history with horses. I do, however, sense that it starts with some level of appreciation and respect for the animal as a being with their own desires and fears, no matter how unsophisticated or easily exploited these may seem in comparison to our own.

In practice, though, this can be treacherous territory to navigate—territory that got stranger and seemingly more dangerous after I fractured my vertebrae, forcing me to recognize how high the stakes were. In fact, I was forced to accept that not finding this balance could result in another injury or death. Harry explains that, as herd animals, horses respond well to clear communication—their instincts demand it—and in the absence of clarity, they are forced to fill in themselves, whether they want to or not.

I was too much the novice with Shoshona, but I can learn to be better with Treasure. I can be his source of support if I find a way to be assertive and clear, to communicate with him effectively. It doesn't mean he'll never experience anxiety when confronted with a new question, but it does mean that I can strive to avoid "cross[ing] into the realm of punishment and creat[ing] too much anxiety that switches off a horse's ability to problem-solve and results in reactions instead of responses" (Jacobs, February 17, 2020). Perhaps this is where we can best strike the balance in guiding our animals to a place that feels safe. Maybe I need to feel Treasure's power and dependence in such nuanced ways in order to understand and remember that these creatures are constantly pulsating with instinct, fear, strength, and attachment—elements of their very nature that aren't meant to be diluted or subjugated by whips and chains, but enhanced and appreciated through a meaningful partnership and through respect. 🐎

Katie

I SLIPPED MY boots on, still a bit stunned as I sorted through what I had just awkwardly discussed with my counselor Angela before arriving at the ranch—the ways I struggle to set boundaries with others, the ways I give too much of myself. Angela told me that this inclination originated with my mother, who has her own struggles with setting boundaries, her own tendency to give everything and get little in return. This conclusion appeared hopeless yet simultaneously unsurprising. Of course I learned these behaviors from my mother! Of course my relationships have taken the path blazed by my parents! Isn't that what everyone figures out in counseling?

As I reached for Treasure's halter hanging loosely on the dusty horseshoe beside his stall, my phone began to ring. Seeing that it was my mother, I hesitated to answer because I knew she would want to talk for a while. I picked up anyway. Immediately, I could hear in her voice the desperation she was trying to conceal. Even through the phone, the ache was palpable. "Ashley, I am so done. I don't know what to do anymore. I am just so tired," she said. On the last word, her voice finally broke, and the way she sniffled into the phone made a crackling noise through the receiver.

As I stood outside the gate, Treasure shifted in his stall impatiently while I responded to my mother's frustration the way I always do when she makes these sorts of comments, the way most children do when they see their parents splinter and split. Playing with the blue-and-black braiding on Treasure's halter, I mumbled half-hearted words of consolation, knowing that as her child, I couldn't fully offer her what she needed to hear. The reality was that my mother had been tired for a long time. Raising two rambunctious boys, one with a cognitive disability, is a monumental undertaking, and I couldn't change that. All I could do was offer her my ear and my support.

I placed the phone back in my pocket and marveled at the timing of my mother's call and the sudden surge in the hopelessness I had already been feeling. When I opened the gate to Treasure's stall, he stepped toward me and gently lowered his head into the halter. As I rubbed his downy coat, which whirled into what looked like a starburst between his large, almond-shaped eyes, I remembered moments like this I'd had with Shoshona, moments in which I sought comfort in the softness of her fur, with its sleek formations and swirls, and in the sturdiness of her body.

As a retired racehorse, Treasure wasn't settled like she was; he was more prone to flight and spookiness. Moments with Treasure were harder to hold at first, and it was harder to relish the stillness and intimacy of quiet. Nothing could fully compare to what I had had as a girl with Shoshona, but Treasure and I were forging a new kind of relationship, and that would be enough. Together, woman and horse, we would find our own path. Plus, the routine—the moments lost in ritual—was part of the comfort.

—

My mother and Erika introduced me to riding. After marrying my father and renting a house that came with property large enough for horses, my mother bought a kind and gentle horse named Katie and learned to barrel race. My mother doesn't talk about it much, and she stopped riding when I was very young, but I like to imagine my mother zipping in and out of the barrels on her pretty bay horse. I like to imagine my mother, bony and slight, becoming powerful and fast from Katie's back, her brilliant blue eyes blazing beneath the brim of her cowboy hat. Shortly after, Erika started riding as well. My grandmother bought her Shoshona, a neglected show horse, and the two began participating in 4-H and competing in local horse shows.

When Shoshona came into Erika's life, she was thin like Treasure was when he entered mine, her bones glaring beneath her dull coat. Shoshona's owner had thrown her into a sparse pasture all alone—punishment for an accident that was in no way Shoshona's fault. The previous owner liked to gallop Shoshona down her long asphalt driveway and pull hard on the reins, ripping the metal bit into Shoshona's mouth, forcing her to rear up into the air like the horses in the movies. One day, Shoshona lost her footing and fell on top of the woman, breaking the woman's hip. Erika and my grandmother saved Shoshona. They made her the horse I fell in love with.

Erika competed in horse shows with Shoshona for a few years before she sold her, along with all of her tack, to my mother—the rich chestnut leather bridle with shiny silver hearts along the edges, the breast collar that draped her strong chest, covered in thick plates of silver and the same hearts as on the bridle. Shoshona also came with some warnings. Having been neglected and beaten in her former life, she had triggers that sometimes set her off. She could also be obstinate. Once, during a jumping competition, Erika was riding Shoshona effortlessly over the first couple of jumps, soaring through the air before galloping toward the next jump. But then, right when she should have jumped, Shoshona planted her feet, pushed the weight of her body into the sudden stop, and lowered her head. She catapulted Erika, who was primed for the jump, over her head and face-first into the dirt. Erika raised her head, putting her hand to her mouth where the stinging had set in, and felt the sharpness where her tooth had chipped during the fall and pierced part of her lip. The soreness had already settled in her shoulders after she skidded across the ground. Shoshona simply stood on the other side of the jump, waiting to be collected and taken out of the arena.

Years later, despite being wary, I would have my own experience with Shoshona refusing a jump. I, too, was competing in a horse show and needed just a few more points for the high-point belt buckle I had coveted, already imagining myself wearing it on my thin black leather belt, embellished with silver hearts to match all of my tack. I needed one more class, but the only ones remaining were more advanced than I was ready for. Having never been over jumps that high or trained in the proper way to approach them, I shouldn't have been competing at that level. At the same time, I needed those final points. I didn't need to do well; I simply needed to be entered to win in overall points. My trainer Carol, who was Erika's former trainer with Shoshona, didn't seem worried and told me it would be fine. She reminded me that Shoshona had been trained over jumps that high before; I only needed to ride it out. I trusted Carol, and more importantly, I trusted Shoshona. I knew that she could do it.

As Shoshona and I smoothly cantered our way through a circle, leaving a perfect trail in the loose dirt, I remained calm and sure of myself. We found our rhythm in the canter, Shoshona tucking her head toward her chest and rounding her back underneath me. We took the curve and headed straight toward the first jump, where I was forced to confront its height. Shoshona maintained her steady canter, and as we drew closer, she picked up speed and surged forward. I didn't know Shoshona needed that speed to take the higher jump, didn't realize she was trying to carry us through it safely, and so the sudden burst of quickness surprised me. My body stopped moving with her, blocking her forward momentum.

Without realizing it, I tightened my hold on the reins, signaling for her to slow down. Her gallop died down to a gentle canter, still quick but not the frightening flash of speed and pulse from before. As we approached the jump, Shoshona planted her feet and stopped, refusing it, just as she had with Erika. I stayed in the saddle because I wasn't poised for the jump as Erika had been. My fear had kept me from committing to it. Quickly, I glanced at my mother and Carol, who stood on the edges of the arena, and searched their faces for some guidance. Making a circling motion with her hand, Carol prompted me to try again. So Shoshona and I made another loop before approaching the jump. Once again, I failed to let her gather the speed she needed to clear it. As an adult, I've learned that in the absence of a strong leader, a horse will fill in because their instincts tell them they must in order to survive. Shoshona was simply filling in for what I lacked.

Erika and my grandmother had already warned me of Carol's harshness before I met her for the first time. They warned me of her tendency to yell and scream, yet they trusted her experience and expertise. My mother and I did, too. And knowing that Erika had weathered the exercises and discipline Carol imposed upon us made me, even at a young age, willing to embrace and approach both with a sort of religious seriousness unseen in my childhood playmates.

Carol was very much a practitioner of traditional forms of horsemanship, expecting the horse to submit to her will. She used harsh bits, spurs, and whips to achieve this arrangement. Even at a young age, I felt it was wrong to revere my horse for her power and beauty all the while stifling her with the stroke of a whip. But this was, and is, the norm in the horse world. Now, as an adult studying horsemanship, I regret not knowing then what I do now about gentler approaches to interacting with horses. I cannot help but compare everything I do with Treasure to what I did with Shoshona, finding fault and guilt in every step.

Although I was trained in traditional horsemanship methods that positioned the horse as submissive, I still viewed Shoshona as a companion; I often sat on the fencepost to watch her graze, or leaned against her in the stall, brushing her coat, memorizing her smell and her body. Shoshona filled a sort of caregiver role. She was the largest horse I'd ever been on, yet somehow, the worry of falling or being harmed never existed for me in those days. It was as though she knew a child was on her back.

So, on the day Carol pulled me from the saddle, ripped the smooth leather reins from my small hands and began beating Shoshona hard across the neck with them before cruelly kicking her on the underside of her belly— what she called an "attitude adjustment"—I began to hate Carol. I hated that I still wanted Carol's approval and that I still admired her toughness, so unabashed, something I had rarely seen in a woman. Most of all, I hated that I was powerless to protect Shoshona the way I felt she protected me. I wished that I were like the feisty heroines in the cowgirl movies who had no problem standing up for themselves or for their horses. But this wasn't a movie, and I was afraid.

Because I loved riding and competing in horse shows with Shoshona, loved feeling strong and capable, and loved the discipline, I stuck with it in spite of Carol. Caring for and riding Shoshona established a steadiness in my life that I needed, particularly through my teen years. My mother, like many mothers in cowgirl stories, raised me to pursue any endeavor that I dreamed up and offered her undying support when I did. So when I decided to play football in the fifth grade, despite there never having been a girl on the team, I thought nothing of it. Why shouldn't I be on the football team? My mother was as excited—and unwitting—as I was. Together, we shopped for a practice jersey and a bag to carry my gear in. We figured out how to put on my pads in the comfort and warmth of our living room.

There was one problem we hadn't anticipated: the boys. They swiftly and overwhelmingly made it clear that I was unwelcome, and no pep talk from my mother could shield me from their vitriol. Often, they cornered me at school, their faces pinched into angry grimaces, to tell me that "girls don't play football." Even my well-meaning coach made me feel as though I didn't belong on the football field no matter how hard I tried. Once, as I walked down the hall lugging my giant football bag over my shoulder, he said, "Wells, you don't look like a football player!" He chuckled as he continued on, while I stood there looking down at the emerald-green crushed-velvet dress my mother had bought me, embarrassed and ashamed for being too feminine, for simply being a girl.

I didn't fare any better on the field. Boys from the other team targeted me for laughs as soon as they heard a girl was on the team. They made it a point to needlessly plow into me. With every taunt, every shove from one of my own teammates or every sneer in my direction, just because I wanted to play alongside the boys, I learned the hard lesson that I wasn't always in control of my space or my body. When I rode Shoshona, I was. In the arena, I possessed an extraordinary power that I didn't have outside of it.

———

Erika and Carol spent hours in the arena with me, calling out corrections to my flaws and form. My mother rose early with me, as the darkness lingered and the stars blinked above, and helped me dress in my show clothes. She pulled my hair into a tight bun, gelled slick and crunchy against my head to fit underneath my cowboy hat, as I sipped at a Pepsi, attempting to shake off the lethargy of sleep. Together, we loaded Shoshona into the trailer and traveled to wherever that day's show was to be held. My grandmother often met us there, sometimes with brightly frosted donuts. The shows I took part in were mostly local 4-H horse shows, but a few drew us further from home. It was special traveling with my mother and my horse through the abandoned streets, while my father and brothers remained at home, tucked up in their beds. Although I loved the crisp mornings spent fishing with my family and the languid evenings playing catch, with that satisfying snap of the ball hitting the glove and my father's laughter floating through the summer air, this was something for my mother and me. Just the two of us.

When I qualified for the state horse competition, I spent weeks preparing and practicing. My mother began measuring me for the show jackets she'd sew especially for the event so I would fit in with the other competitors who'd be wearing the gaudy, sparkling jackets typical in western competitions. Wandering through fabric stores, we fingered the slick and shiny satins—deep blues, elegant greens, stunning blood reds, and the lace with its intricate patterns—as we considered which colors would be the most eye-catching when paired with Shoshona's gray coat. Leading up to the competition, my mother spent late nights hunched over the sewing machine, her hair pinned back from her face to free her hands and eyes, as my brothers, my father, and I slept. Eventually, we grew oblivious to the stop and start of the machine, to the needle humming away into the night. As we loaded the truck with our luggage for the trip, I carefully carried my new shimmering jackets, lined up on their hangers. I noticed that inside each one, my mother had affixed a little patch that read: "Handmade with love by mom."

When I was young, people always commented on the close resemblance between my father and me—mostly in our eyes. I'm the only child with my father's brown eyes; my brothers have the dazzling blue eyes of our mother. My father and I continue to share many traits—our humor, sturdiness, and emotional reserve, but my mother needs me in ways that he never will. For that reason, I feel an intimacy with my mother that is at times hard to explain. When Shoshona died and I was no longer homebound, I told my mother that I was thinking about applying to graduate schools in other states. We sat on the patio of my parents' home, warmed by the sun, and she paused for a moment. "But who will help me with your brothers?" she asked. I understood her concern, and I also understood that she was not being selfish. Although I am her daughter, I sometimes filled the role of partner and supporter, too—a sort of stand-in caregiver for my little brothers.

Normally, the ways in which my mother needs me emerge clear and distinct: She gives of herself the way I tend to, and she suffers for it in ways that I worry about. Which is why on the rare occasion that my mother dispenses advice, I take it.

Like when Jake and I were falling apart. We'd been together for five years, and one weekend after he'd left town for a visit with his family, I stood in my mother's kitchen discussing the state of our relationship. I told her about his coldness and pettiness, the resentment that dripped from the words spoken between us. Most talks with my mother happen in the kitchen as she flutters about scrubbing or cooking. I leaned on my elbows against the cool, smooth tile as she stood across from me, taking a sip from her glass of chardonnay. Seeing in her face that she was considering something but didn't want to speak it, I prompted her.

"What? What is it?" I asked.

She hesitated a few seconds before finally saying, "Break up with him, Ashley. You need to be with someone that supports you."

After leaving that night, I agonized over her words as I drove the dark streets to the empty apartment I shared with Jake. I knew they were birthed of her experiences, our shared experiences, and therefore carried a certain weight that I could not ignore. Later, as I sat on the steps of my apartment drinking beer and recounting the advice to a couple of friends, they reminded me of a party the weekend prior when Jake had made fun of my smile in front of everyone, calling me "horse face." I searched out confirmation and support from my friends as we talked well into the night; I wanted to hear the actual words— *leave him*—over and over again so I could justify ending our five years together. But I knew in my gut that the only words I really *needed* to hear were my mother's.

The next day, I visited a local animal shelter, hoping to adopt a kitten, something Jake forbade me from doing. As I made my way through the small room containing stacks of metal cages filled with young cats, my father called. Ignoring the ringing in my purse, I poked my index finger through the bars to stroke their fur and the raised bridges between their eyes. I was bursting with defiance that morning when I walked through the doors of the shelter, but I left crushed and dejected, discouraged by the pathetic mewing and by my inability to save them. They could never offer me the comfort that I sought.

Not like Shoshona could. Since Shoshona's death two years before, I'd been searching—unsuccessfully—for that sureness and mutuality of being able to care for something wholeheartedly, without resentment and anger interfering.

Standing outside the shelter, pressing my shoes into the wet dirt lining the planters, I returned my father's call. "I hear you and Jake are having problems," he said. "Break up with him, Ashley. He's a jerk." I took his words to heart, certainly, but not in the same way as my mother's. My father takes care of me and can always detect the hurt I try to hide. I go to him when I need help, but he lacks the experience of someone who gives too much of themselves, as women so often do. My mother's words ached. They held history and proof in them. Erika was also enlisted by my mother to speak to me. As she explained her own struggles with her husband—the distance, the loneliness, the desire to get out—I trusted her.

Around the same time I began questioning my relationship with Jake, I started yearning to be in the saddle again. I didn't feel like myself without a horse. It was as though I'd lost my strength and bearings in the world, and my failing relationship with Jake only served to exacerbate those feelings of weakness and compromise. My pledge to Shoshona had kept me steady, and I could rely on it to be there and to be uncomplicated in a way that I couldn't on anything else. I was lost without that devotion as it had been there for most of my life.

Meeting and riding with Jennifer helped me to begin reconciling the person I'd lost with the person I'd started to become, slowly building my strength and confidence again as we wandered the trails blazed by deer on their magically thin legs. Although I was on a borrowed horse, the rides reminded me of Shoshona. As we rode deeper into the brush and trees with their low-hanging branches and leaves with lacy veins, we were far from home, but I hardly noticed because on those rides, I began to feel more found than I had since Shoshona's death. Jennifer and Cody reminded me of what a relationship with horses and with nature meant for my life and well-being. At twenty-five, spending so much time out on the trail with Jennifer, I allowed her to fill the role of a guide and model for how I wanted my life to be. Out there, I realized just how far my life with Jake had strayed from where I had imagined we might end up.

Jake had constantly resisted my devotion to Shoshona. He didn't—nor did he ever really try to—understand my intense loyalty to an animal. Although some of my girlfriends didn't understand what it was like to love a horse like I loved Shoshona, they at least tried. And I was moved by their effort. When I returned home from having Shoshona euthanized, aching and alone, I found a small bouquet of flowers leaning against the sliding glass door, with a tiny note buried among the petals. My best friend Emma, who'd entered my life years before Jake and would remain long after, had left it for me, knowing

I would need something pretty and delicate and tender when I returned. The softness of the petals, and their smoothness and color, were a comfort. They weren't meant to ease the ache—she knew that couldn't happen, at least not so soon, but they acted as something I could hold and care for fleetingly.

That night, Jake came home from work after I had cried in the shower for an hour. I was dozing on the couch, exhausted and drained, when he sat on the edge of a cushion and offered me a box of chocolates he'd picked up on his way home. In that moment, I appreciated the gesture, the act of kindness, but still, it somehow felt cheap—too convenient, with the candy shop being across the street from his work; too easy, he having overlooked the fact that I don't really like sweets. I wanted so badly to be thankful, to believe that after years of resenting Shoshona and what she represented, Jake was finally ready to try and understand why I was hurting. I wanted to believe he could help carry some of the weight, but I knew that he simply couldn't. He would never understand what it was about a girl and her horse that was special. 🐎

Black Beauty

JENNIFER AND I planned our trail-riding trip to the mountains for months. Although we had our own horses, we were to ride rented ones so we could scope out the area and come back later. I had been hesitant, knowing that the horses on guided trips are typically trained with the traditional techniques—reliant on submission and domination—that I'd been trying to distance myself from, recognizing that paying to ride one made me a hypocrite. Still, I had some grotesque need to remind myself of traditional horsemanship's faults and the harm that occurs when money becomes involved, to bear witness somehow. I considered this as Jennifer and I drove through the narrow, winding roads, climbing toward the mountain we'd be riding around.

A few trucks were already parked in the dirt lot under the massive pine tree. People in tennis shoes and jeans milled about waiting for the ride to start, their consent forms already signed and filed away. The guides sat around an empty fire pit, laughing and telling jokes. Each of them looked young, maybe just out of—and some still attending—high school. One stared hard in my direction, and his eyes burned into me as he scanned my body.

As we waited for the others in our group to arrive, Jennifer and I strolled past the horses tied to the hitching post, stopping to rub each wide forehead. The horses' eyelids drooped as they stood there, bored, being part of an unwavering routine. It reminded me of the horse shows I went to as a child and a teen. Old leather saddles sat atop their backs awkwardly, stiff and ill-shaped, as if they'd been left out in the sun too long. Some of their hooves were chipped and cracked, and I wondered why they were being ridden through hard and rocky terrain on hooves that were in such poor shape. I already knew the answer: It was their job. Jennifer also noticed how pitiful each of the horses looked, being tied there day after day, lugging people through the mountains, and she turned to me and whispered, "These poor horses."

One of the guides rang a bell attached to the side of the old barn; the loud, tinny sound alerted us that it was time for the ride to begin. The girl up front knew that Jennifer and I were seasoned equestrians and asked, "Who's more experienced? This guy needs a confident rider." I told her I didn't mind riding him, and she explained that he often reached for bits of green grass and weeds poking out along the trail and ignored less assertive riders. As she spoke, I knew the horse ignored them because he had to in order to cope with the slew of novice riders sending him foggy messages. To survive the nag of miscommunication and ultimately his life as a horse of utility, he had learned to ignore.

Jennifer and I were placed in the back of the line of riders, with a guide pulling up the rear. He was young, with dark brown curls peeking from under his cowboy hat that made him look even younger. He rode his own horse and seemed eager to show off for other riders and to impress Jennifer and me. With a click and a swift kick to his horse's ribs, he galloped up small inclines on the horse before tugging hard on the reins, the bit jamming into the horse's mouth, to turn and rejoin the group. The whites of his horse's eyes flashed each time the boy did this. Ahead of me was a young woman wearing shorts and flip-flops. Her bony feet kept inching further and further into the stirrups, and the guide called out for her to fix them, warning that with her feet jammed so far she could get dragged behind the horse should she fall. I wondered aloud why she was allowed to ride while wearing flip-flops in the first place, but without having to give it much thought, Jennifer quickly answered, "Money." I knew she was right.

My horse dragged his feet, walking crooked and wobbly beneath me for the entire ride. He was only marginally interested in the world around us, lifting his head slightly when children on a picnic near the lake with their parents squealed and burst out of the trees to escape a swarm of bees. The rest of the ride, his head hung low, and he followed the horse in front of him, having memorized the path after months—maybe years—of repeated steps. Back at the barn, I dismounted and handed the reins to one of the guides, who took my horse to join the others in a row. They were already dozing as they waited for the next group of riders, their dull eyes hidden under heavy lids.

Oddly, riding that rented horse reminded me of the high-dollar western pleasure horses who are ridden in the more prestigious competitions—not because of a resemblance in monetary worth or in appearance, given his lackluster coat and cracked hooves. Something in the rented horse's tired movements, however, conjured up the show horses I'd seen in my youth. In theory, western pleasure is supposed to reflect a calm and collected horse, one who is fit and responsive to the rider and who looks like a pleasure to ride, as the name suggests.

Somewhere along the way, though, calm began to mean completely submissive and dull, something resembling lethargy. In an effort to show that the horse wasn't rushing forward, running off with their rider, trainers began insisting on slower movements, mistaking slower for present and responsive. Or more accurately, they simply preferred the easy fix to actually helping the horse feel relaxed and focused. Everything about this style of riding and training horses, down to the way their bodies are changed and formed to fit a particular look, is artificial.

Despite protest in the larger horse community, the way the western pleasure horse holds her head has begun to take on an unnatural form. In nature, when a horse is worried or troubled, her head will shoot high into the air. But in the western pleasure world, training methods have resulted in heads dropping lower and lower, regardless of where the horse is mentally, resulting in a false display of tranquility. This is a position achieved through straps and leverage and cruel backyard methods. Some trainers will strap a horse into a contraption that allows the reins to put added leverage on the horse's mouth and head. Others will tie a horse to a ring high above them so the horse's head is completely outstretched to encourage exhaustion of the neck muscles, resulting in a low-hanging head once the horse is finally released—sometimes not until the next day. Still others may starve their horses into submission and lethargy to achieve those shuffling gaits. Those in the larger community who criticize this style of western horsemanship argue that it should return to its roots. But these lifeless horses, creations of man's heavy hand, remain.

When I was a teenager, my 4-H leader took a group of us to the American Paint Horse Association World Championship Show in Texas. As I strolled through the grounds, stopping at vendor booths, I discovered horse-hair extensions for the first time. Long, shiny locks in a variety of colors hung from a large wood panel. I ran my fingers through them, feeling the smooth strands between my thumb and forefinger. This was my first time watching a competition of this level, and I'd never seen such extreme measures taken to achieve a certain look in a horse. Later, I'd learn that not only do they put fake hair in a show horse's tail, they may also paralyze it with an injection to kill the nerves—what is called "blocking the tail"—because excessive tail swishing or movement signals an unhappy horse.

When the mounted classes began, I took my seat on the bleachers with the others in my group, and we watched the horses and riders file in slowly. Every horse had their head hung low, below their withers. Riders held loosely draped reins. The horses walked slowly, listlessly—unlike Shoshona or most horses at my much lower level of competition. When the announcer called for a jog, the gaits barely changed. As horses and riders shuffled past where I sat, I saw that each horse's eye looked dull and lifeless—blank. The announcer then called for a canter, and their movements were stunted. To an untrained eye, it would appear as if every horse in the arena were hurt and limping.

When I was showing Shoshona, Carol suggested I sell her and buy a horse better suited for western pleasure, a horse who was slower, less animated, one who cost far more than my rescue mare trained by my aunt. We had gone as far as we could in the show circuit, and in order to compete in the more prestigious shows, I would need a better horse. I flatly refused. Selling Shoshona was never an option. Even if it had been affordable to purchase a more advanced horse, even if I hadn't felt committed to that horse and didn't have a relationship with them, even if I believed they were just a means to achieving my personal goals, I couldn't bring myself to ride a horse who seemed so dejected and worn down. I loved Shoshona for her spirit, for the life that glowed in her eyes. And I was satisfied participating in the smaller shows if it meant I could retain that.

That isn't to say that I, as a child, didn't feel the pressure to ask Shoshona to slow down, to drop her head, to ask her body to do something it wasn't meant to do. I did. Usually, I simply bumped the reins lightly with my fingers, and she'd soften. But once, I used a more extreme approach as we prepared for a show, an approach that today, with a fuller understanding of horsemanship, I would never consider. Stringing a set of reins from the girth around Shoshona's stomach through the rings on the bit in her mouth to my hands, I had enough leverage to force Shoshona's head down. Although rationally, I know I shouldn't be so hard on myself since I didn't know any better at the time, I am, in hindsight, deeply ashamed of having done that to my beloved mare. I am ashamed of having forced her into submission.

Despite my regrets, when I look back on the horse shows of my childhood, I don't remember particularly liking the fuss and the falseness, the attention to appearances. But I was attracted to the ritual and routine. Riding in preparation for these competitions, I felt as if Shoshona and I were working toward a purpose—to earn or accomplish something together. I especially liked the quiet hours I spent grooming her. Through the intimacy of the act, the aloneness and quiet, I felt close to her. I was an anxious child, often spending hours before bed fretting over the minutiae of my day. The glow of my nightlight illuminated a poster of a unicorn I had affixed to my closet door across from the bed. On those late nights, I'd stare at that unicorn with her bright white coat and gravity-defying, flowing mane; I'd memorize the tiny details, from the pale green filigree framing her body, frozen and graceful, to the delicate shape of her hooves. This nightly routine calmed me, allowing me to slow my thoughts and capture sleep.

Grooming Shoshona, too, was a practice akin to self-soothing. In those early years, brushing her coat until it shone, massaging her skin with the rubber curry comb, keeping her tail clean and free of tangles—these, to me, were acts of appreciation verging on worship. I liked the way she looked when her coat glinted in the sunlight, when the grooves of her muscles shone, highlighting the things I most valued in her—strength and power. Now, when I reflect on those acts of care, I know that it wasn't simply about preparing for a show or caring for a horse. I cannot help but think of them as a celebration of what Shoshona represented for me as a young girl—freedom, strength, and beauty. A memorization, a recitation of what I wanted to grow up to be.

I washed Shoshona the day before each show. I began by scrubbing out the grass stains on her coat with a white-enhancing shampoo. She stood patiently as I worked the purple shampoo through her tail. As I did this, I thought of the scene in the film *The Wizard of Oz* in which the dyed horses prance across the screen. When I rinsed Shoshona, the purple turned a lavender shade until it washed away altogether. Next, I ran my hands over her coat, scraping the excess water off her in swift, efficient movements before drying her with a towel. Standing behind her, I braided Shoshona's long, thick tail the way my mother taught me, the way she braided my own hair before school. Taking the clippers from their case, I plugged them in and lightly ran them buzzing under her chin, over her muzzle, inside her ears, and carefully down her narrow, bony legs until they met the hooves. I cleared away all the straggly hairs until Shoshona looked as sleek and chiseled as the figurines I collected.

—

Horses have long been creatures of work—used for war, sport, hunting, transportation, and farming. All have traditionally been the domain of men, but the roles that horses play in these activities—as trophy, commodity, or status symbol—are similar to the roles that women play. This is partly why women feel such a unique and compelling attraction to horses. We recognize a sense of sameness in the way our bodies are used, in the paradox of being both tamed and untamed. In *Dark Horses and Black Beauties: Animals, Women, A Passion*, Melissa Holbrook Pierson sums up this paradoxical relationship beautifully:

> They are a stirringly impossible mixture of power and delicacy, size and fragility. They inspire fear even as they are filled with it themselves. They are wild and they are utterly tamable. . . . [H]orses seem to bear the same secret a little girl does about her own protean qualities even if the whole world would deny them. (15)

Perhaps the reason why I could never consider selling Shoshona or imagine discarding her was because wildness still lingered beneath the veneer of domestication and tameness—that sense of wildness made me love her even more.

American rodeo perfectly captures this paradox. In their limited role following the ban, women have exhibited grit, might, and athleticism in barrel racing as well as some other competitions. This is empowering for many young girls, particularly as Black, Indigenous, and (all) women of color reclaim space for themselves in a multi-million-dollar, white-male-dominated industry.

The Cowgirls of Color rodeo team has been highlighted in several mainstream media outlets like *The Cut*, *Dazed*, and *The Guardian*, providing opportunity for team members to share what competing with their horses means for them, which is significant given that the sport systematically shoved Black, Indigenous, and women of color from the arena.

In *Huffington Post*'s "Listen to America" series featuring the Cowgirls of Color and their horses, the women's responses reflect the kind of intersectional approach that is shamefully missing from the horse industry. The women describe the usual feelings—of confidence, friendship, fearlessness—when it comes to their horses, but they also speak to access and racism. Pennie, a team member who started the STAND Foundation, which provides horse experiences to inner-city youths in Washington D.C., states, "This world that we live in, to me, really is not designed for our kids to even be successful." To provide opportunity for Black youth to spend time in nature with horses, then, is huge. Although the Bill Pickett Invitational Rodeo is a site for Black cowboys and cowgirls to enjoy the sport, the overall access and whiteness have troubled me since I joined the horse world anew as an adult with Treasure. At the same time, I am not blind to the rodeo's abundant cruelty, from the harsh spurs to the pain inflicted on cows and horses expressly for show. But it isn't always this way between woman and horse, and that strikes at the heart of the ambivalence for me.

Once, as we sat around the table eating breakfast one morning at his clinic in Arizona, Harry related to us stories from his days in the rodeo. He told us about watching the women in a barrel-racing competition, and about one day in particular. Women on stout and muscular horses took turns bursting through the gates, the horses' legs pumping fiercely as the women brought the pointed ends of the reins down hard on their horses' rumps in swift successions. The pairs whipped in and out of the barrels in a clover formation, each seeking the best time.

Harry said that one horse and one rider stood out to him among the frenzied pairs. As the woman and her horse sped around the arena, her steed lacked the frantic, harsh look the others wore. To him, the horse and rider seemed to have achieved a certain harmony between them, so much so that he wandered through the grounds looking for the rider at the end of the competition. Approaching the woman, he said, "You use this horse for something other than barrel racing, don't you?" The woman looked at him and said, "He's the horse I use on the ranch. I use him for everything." As he told the story, Harry leaned back a little in his chair and explained the point: The rider and her horse had a relationship achieved through a common goal. By being clear that they had a job to do, together, the woman and her horse had come to achieve the sense of mutuality I wanted with my own.

Before hearing this story and learning from Harry, who is one of the gentlest horsepeople I've encountered, I had only seen relationships with working horses that relied on techniques of submission and domination. I had only seen whips, chains, heavy bits, and devices all used as equalizers to make up for our physical smallness next to these large animals. I had only seen relationships based on force when horses were used for a job. In the week after he told that story, Harry showed us that we could complete a job with our horses while retaining their integrity.

After all, this was how the history between horses and humans began—a relationship born of purpose and need. Our horses could be treated like animals with vibrant spirits, the pulse of instinct existing within them, and still help us succeed in our endeavors. It didn't have to be one or the other. There needn't be a sacrifice. "You can break a horse," writes Melissa Holbrook Pierson. "You can humble him with violence and shackle him until he submits. You can meet 'disobedience' with a quick whip." Or, she posits, you can try empathy. Holbrook Pierson adds: "Empathy is not an idea that sells well to the bulk of humanity, particularly if it is directed toward nonhumans" (123).

Ross Jacobs, a horsemanship practitioner I've worked with, describes this as "training to high levels of focus, clarity, and softness." It's helping a horse be okay with what we ask because we ask in a way that makes the horse feel like it "came from inside and not from pure obedience." Now, this is different from enjoying a job, which, according to Jacobs, requires that we "find what job or discipline it [*sic*] feels happiest doing." This poses a challenge for many horsepeople. We can be so quick to project our will onto the horse that we see excitement where there is angst, desire where there is anxiety.

I've heard some people complain that when they are too busy to ride, their horses need a job, as if they are missing out on something that they require, when their "job" in the wild is vastly different from the jobs we've assigned them. In the wild, their job is to survive, eat, and reproduce. Their job is not to drag cattle writhing behind them, or to pull a carriage, or to circle an arena, or to carry us down a trail. These are not their jobs but ours. Throughout history, we've asked everything of our horses. We've asked them to remain with us no matter how difficult the task, no matter how terrifying. We've asked them to charge into battle donning all the armaments of war, from cold, heavy metal to gas masks. We've worn them down until they were nothing more than sagging flesh and bone. We've asked far too much of them and offered very little in return.

Horses still remain among the most abused domesticated animals. Anna Sewell's quintessential horse book, *Black Beauty*, draws attention to the devastating cruelties horses face. There's something significant about crafting the "autobiography" of Black Beauty, about writing a book of this nature, one from the perspective of a horse. This perspective is so often missing from the cowgirl narratives; if it weren't, perhaps we'd be better at actually seeing the horse for who they are. While there are certainly cartoons and books taking the horse's perspective, they don't tackle cruelty in the same way Sewell does in her 1877 novel.

Sewell argues that a horse depends on the kindness of their caretaker to handle them responsibly, which was an important call to action at the time and remains something we in the horse world continue to struggle with. One need look no further than the Tennessee Walking Horse competitions to see what's been done to horses in order to achieve the "big lick" gait. Despite— or because of—impotent legislation with little funding for enforcement, soring, the practice of applying caustic agents to a horse's legs with the sole intent of causing pain, remains routine. Trainers who have flagrantly ignored the law continue to be rewarded within the industry. Because horses occupy the gray area between livestock and companion animal, average conventions of a discipline, like the padded shoes Tennessee Walkers are forced to perform in and the unnatural tail set, can be explained away, no matter how barbaric they may be.

Most of us have good intentions when we work with our horses, job or no job. Yet we still fall short, and simply acknowledging this can be controversial in horse communities. Events at the European Dressage

Championships in the Netherlands in 2019 demonstrate this stark reality. Competitor and triple Olympic gold medalist Charlotte Dujardin was disqualified because she drew blood from her horse's flank—a violation of the Fédération Equestre Internationale's "no blood" rule. In a post, Ross Jacobs rightfully points out the absurdity that such a rule must exist in a discipline that originated as the standard for softness, responsiveness, and grace. If competitors at that level, whose performance should be the consummation of skill, cannot ride without drawing blood from the mouth or the body of their horses, he asks, what are we rewarding?

Just as money and sponsorships have pervaded other horse disciplines, they have transformed the sport. The effects trickle down to amateur competitors. Based on the comments, Jacobs's post criticizing the use of force and arguing for reform, out of the love for the horse, appears to be one of his most controversial. Many rushed to defend Dujardin. Jacobs's viewpoint remains the exception rather than the rule in the broader horse community. In fact, a friend of mine who is firmly of the views of the dressage world calls my work with Treasure hocus-pocus, never mind the fact that I can do things with him—such as ride bitless, ride outside alone, and dress wounds—that she can't with her high-dollar yet reactive horse.

We in the horse world can be quick to passionately object to slaughtering wild horses or soring, but we're less willing to criticize what is happening in front of our eyes. We like to think our approaches to equine husbandry have grown more humane, broadly speaking. However, that doesn't mean we aren't harming our horses deeply when we train for obedience only. And it doesn't mean that we shouldn't be seeking out better ways to exist with our equine partners, who give us everything they have despite the abuses we've historically piled upon them. So many horses, at all levels and in all disciplines, are obedient—graceful, agile, and fast—but are racked by emotional turmoil. Shouldn't we hope for more? I'm starting to understand this as I struggle with my own complicity, as I try to reconcile the person I was—a young girl who, despite her best intentions and despite an intense love, at times treated her horse in ways that she was not proud of—with the person I am now— an adult trying to nurture a relationship with her new horse, one that is more like a partnership, that entails working with and respecting his spirit.

Pete

CANDACE AND I met at her ranch early in the morning; a spring chill lingered in the air and dew clung to the grass, making everything damp and fresh. After loading her trailer with our tack and feed and hoisting our suitcases into the back seat of her truck, Candace and I were ready for the horses. I walked out to the pasture, where a herd of geldings, including our own, was spread out over the five acres of tall grass, heads lowered to the ground and munching quietly. We had spent the past few weeks preparing our horses for the trip from Fresno to Salome, Arizona, to attend a horsemanship clinic with Harry Whitney. We'd added salt to the horses' food to help them hydrate, the chiropractor's nimble fingers and strong hands had made adjustments, and a farrier had trimmed their hooves into clean rounds to be able to withstand the rocky desert terrain. Yet as I made my way out to Treasure and Candace's horse, Pete, I wondered about the abruptness of leaving and of the transition they'd experience, grazing with the herd one minute and being loaded into the trailer the next. The strangeness of being entirely unaware of what was about to happen, of having no concept of travel or goodbye.

Pete and Treasure calmly entered the trailer and poked their noses through the bars, inhaling the spring air through their large flared nostrils, their velvety muzzles vibrating softly with each deep breath. I felt awkward and a little worried about the twelve-hour drive ahead of us. Although Candace and I got along at the ranch and talked often, we didn't actually know each other very well and were decades apart in age. I, a chronic worrier, anticipated the inevitable lull in conversation, the moment we would run out of horse-related topics and I would have to acknowledge the lull and reach into my bag and pull out a book or my iPod. Candace admitted later that night at dinner that she'd worried about the very same thing.

However, as we sped along the highway, the words came easily and the radio remained silent. We fell in with the flow of big rigs and cars and discussed everything from barn gossip to our mothers, relationships with men, and even spirituality. In the side mirror, I watched Pete poke his nose through the bars, assessing his place and inhaling the new smells of the road, as Treasure stood contentedly behind him. As I watched the horses, Candace described her struggle with her mother, the ways her mother pushed and tried to control her. Her words seemed to move with the rhythm and hum of the tires, and she never took her kind blue eyes off the road. She spoke unwaveringly, revealing the brand of confidence that comes with age—a sureness I admired. The way she spoke of her mother and being taken advantage of reminded me of Jake and what I'd accepted in our five years together. I told her about how I was seeing a counselor to deal with boundary problems, with my struggle to set and keep them.

—

I remember taking a trip with Jake and his family for Thanksgiving. We were sipping sake in the small lobby of the Japanese-inspired hotel his mother had booked for us all to stay at, and the light felt soft and comfortable. Since we were sitting in a nook, everything felt intimate despite the buzz of other guests socializing. Jake's mother leaned forward as she spoke.

"So, Ashley, how did you get to all those horse shows? Your dad didn't mind taking you all over the place?"

We'd been discussing the horse competitions of my childhood and teen years, the countless Saturdays I spent at ranches and fairgrounds, being in the heat and sun all day and returning home caked in dirt and sweat.

"Oh, my mom took me to almost all of them. The ones she couldn't, my aunt and grandma did," I said, careful to hide any surprise at or criticism of her assumption that handling a large animal and driving a truck and trailer had to have been done by my father.

"That must be where you get it from," she said, looking satisfied as she crossed her arms and leaned back in her chair, as if she'd solved some great mystery, as if everything made sense now.

I've been aligned with my father for years, yet I've come to understand that I am, in deep and complicated ways, my mother's daughter, formed by a coven of sisters and mothers who taught me the value of companionship with other women through the tracings of their lives. They birthed in me an abiding interest in horses, leading me to develop friendships with a couple of women much older than me, including Candace. These are horse-centered relationships that I cherish and that have irrevocably altered my path as a horsewoman.

Over the years, I've come to understand that my relationships with other horsewomen are significant with regard to my relationship with horses and nature. In a literal way, Candace and other women from our barn made my time at Harry's possible as I couldn't afford a truck or trailer of my own, ushering me into this horsemanship community that I've found a home in. But more than that, they recognize the challenges in sustaining a commitment to this type of work, offering support as I grapple with ideas and failures. Although the nuances may change, there is something sparkling and meaningful about the kind of camaraderie between women that has horses at the center. I've experienced the ways we gain strength through that camaraderie and through our horses, through the gentle yet sure guidance we learn to practice as part of our skills. As a woman in this world, I've encountered versions of the same domination—that claustrophobic oppression of me, controlling my space—that horses must endure when all of their options are taken away. In these female-dominated spaces, we can openly acknowledge the smallness we learn at work, school, or home. And we work together to dismantle it.

—

As we, two women together, covered all of those miles with our horses, I savored our independence, our ability to leave our homes for the wideness of the desert, the freedom to wander with our horses. Not even the seedy truck drivers leering at us as we passed by could ruin it, although they came close. Growing up, I always looked forward to driving near the trucks, to pumping my arms wildly and the bellowing honk that usually followed. Now that I'm an adult, though, the road feels more sinister as I've run into problems with truck drivers the last few times I've driven out of state with another woman. I've heard the stories, the unfair generalizations, and have resisted believing them. But each time Candace and I drew near a truck and found ourselves parallel to the compact steel cab carrying the male driver, I stared out my window and caught another gaze that, despite my over a decade of being cat-called, unnerved me and made me feel dirty. It made me feel as if the powerful space Candace and I had created together could be intruded upon by a mere look.

Stopping for snacks and the bathroom, we pulled into the bumpy dirt lot near the gas station, beside a neat row of big rigs. I ignored the man who whinnied at us between filthy cupped hands, checked on Treasure and Pete, and walked into the gas station. After stocking up on snacks—guilty-pleasure food for the road, I noticed a small girl standing near the trailer looking up at the horses inside. She was mesmerized, her mother's calls from the gas pump unacknowledged. Candace asked if she would like to pet the horses, and the girl nodded, smiling shyly. She ran her tiny fingers up and down Pete's flat forehead and touched the exquisite smoothness of his muzzle. She seemed stunned for a moment—as I'd been the first time I felt the surprising tenderness of a horse—before she returned to her mother's car, leaving a light trail of dust in her wake.

Candace handed me the keys. "It's pretty straight from this point forward—just desert," she said. "You'll be fine." I had never hauled a trailer before and immediately imagined it overturning, leaving a mess of delicate legs jumbled and twisted together, and mauled horse bodies sprawled on the side of the road among a heap of metal. I was hauling not only my own horse but also Candace's, adding to the pressure. But I buried my nervousness, knowing I'd need to do this at some point. I climbed into the driver's seat and began adjusting the mirrors. As I pressed my foot to the gas pedal and we crept over the potholes and dips in the lot, the weight of the trailer and the two horses became more real to me, more tangible.

The grape orchards of the Central Valley gave way to empty spaces, golden and sprawling, spattered with the occasional patch of delicate violet wildflowers not yet burned away by the desert sun. I felt charmed driving down the highway lined with rocks and cacti. Ocotillo bushes, with their spindly branches and bright red flowers, sprawled and stretched across the blue like fingers pointing and directing us onward. Wide mountains spread before us, sprinkled with gray boulders. All of that nothingness felt peaceful, even beautiful, and brought with it a sense of ease in its sturdiness.

Sometimes, it looked like the backdrop of a movie, especially when we passed through seemingly abandoned towns, with a scattering of small apartment buildings and cacti growing among boarded-up businesses. I imagined a gunfight in the middle of the empty streets. Or some wayward wanderer smoking a cigarette against the side of one of the empty stores, smoke twirling around greasy hair matted with sweat from the desert heat. As we passed through, I watched a teenaged girl in cutoff denim shorts and a pink t-shirt stand alone in the middle of a barren field, flying a brightly colored kite in the shape of a butterfly.

———

Aside from that of the Canadian couple living and studying with Harry for the spring, our truck was the first to crawl down the gravel road that was used only by vehicles entering the heart of the desert and lost travelers seeking a place to turn around and return to whence they came, to get back on track. Dusk billowed around us, lightly blurring the edges of the mountains that hours ago had seemed so far away, softening the brilliant sun. Pete and Treasure had their muzzles pressed through the bars, investigating this new place by the smell of it. Pete had been to Harry's forty-five-acre ranch before, and Candace wondered aloud whether he remembered it by the scent, the dryness.

After I walked Treasure out of the trailer, his head lifted straight into the air, the muscles in his neck stretched and taut. He pushed against me with his heavy shoulder, stepping into my space, and I worried for a few moments that he would bolt and I would lose him. His eyes looked wild as they scanned the new scenery. Quietly at first, I asked him to step out of my space by softly wiggling the lead rope. As we approached the turnout, I noticed that it was all rock and gravel with a few lone cacti. Treasure had never been on such rocky and uneven terrain, and I wondered how my retired racehorse, accustomed to smoothly manicured tracks and wide flat pastures, would do in this new climate. I wondered how I would do, too, expecting the aloneness of the desert and of the trip to set in and make me ache for home. That ache never came.

I rubbed Treasure's forehead and ears. Candace said goodnight to Pete as well before we removed their halters and left them to explore this unfamiliar space. Treasure and Pete hesitantly set their hooves down on the rocks beneath them, as if on tiptoes, and carefully navigated their way down the uneven hill toward the hay we'd set out for them on the smoothest, flattest section of the turnout. Candace and I both worried that the change in place would upset Treasure, would build in him a sense of unease that would be hard to redirect and refocus in the week to come.

But there wasn't much time for us to worry about the horses after reaching the bunkhouse. The others started to trickle in—women from all over the country, and two husbands along for the ride. In my experience, it usually works out this way, with mostly women at these clinics. Scanning the pictures on the walls, I saw very few male faces aside from Harry's. Broad smiles and eagerness for the week ahead turned the room charged and electric, especially once Harry sauntered in, looking every bit like a cowboy from the movies, dressed in a pressed shirt with pearl buttons, denim vest, and jeans tucked into tall, intricately stitched cowboy boots. He walked with a hint of a bow-legged cowboy swagger and seated himself at the head of the long table covered with a red gingham tablecloth, and we all gathered around to begin introductions and discuss goals for the week. Harry joked with the husbands about finally having some men around. Though few of us had known each other before the clinic, around the table there was a feeling of warmth, of community built upon a common goal and interest, of a willingness to support one another. The stars hung brightly in the vast sky.

Early the following morning, I woke to the unexpected and zealous squawking of a bird outside our window. Whenever I'd thought of the desert, I'd imagined stillness, quiet. But over the week with Harry, I found myself surprised by the many animals—rodents, birds, snakes—who were active and scurrying about day and night, by the life constantly pulsing through the heat and rock and open space. Burying myself deeper within the softness of my sleeping bag, I tried to ignore the bird's calls, but he was relentless. I wandered out of the bunkhouse and saw Candace walking down the gravel hill, leading one horse on each side. Treasure marched along, calm and steady. "Look at your newly empowered steed," Candace said to me, beaming, as she handed off the lead rope. And she seemed to be right. His eyes were relaxed, his head lowered, neck softly sloping. Realizing he was not being sold off or expected to compete in yet another stressful race at a different location, Treasure had developed a newfound confidence almost overnight.

Harry is often lumped in with the natural horsemanship movement because he emphasizes working with the horse's thought and retaining the integrity of the horse—their spirit, unlike traditional approaches that rely on domination through fear, on punishment, whips and chains, quick fixes with no meaning behind them and no clear message. Working with the horse's thought involves being clear on intent and paying close attention to the energy you are putting out. Horses in the wild—feral horses in the U.S.—function in their herds and communicate very clearly among themselves because their survival depends on it. They bite, kick, and neigh, but behind the gestures, there's neither real anger nor an intent to instill blind fear.

Building a partnership with your horse—a sense of being herd-bound—creates a confidence and trust that often aren't possible using traditional approaches that hinge upon obedience. According to Tom Moates in his book *A Horse's Thought*, which draws from his work with Harry, "If the horse doesn't find us dependable, trustworthy, assertive, or consistent then the confidence they need to follow and trust in is simply not going to be there." It's about clarity, which, as Moates explains, is a big responsibility.

I hadn't considered instinct when I had Shoshona. I was too young, too immersed in traditional forms of horsemanship, and too invested in the image of Shoshona as a friend and an ideal to understand that she was simply an animal guided by instincts and the need to survive. In my young self's mind, Shoshona's actions were her taking care of me. Now, I realize that she lacked a confident leader, and her instincts prompted her to fill in to survive.

Shortly before Shoshona's death, Jake and I were sitting on the couch in our condo, eating pizza and watching PBS. Featuring lush shots saturated with vivid greens, the film follows a herd of wild horses galloping across the grassy plains, their manes wild and knotted. One of the mares, a little red one, gives birth to a foal, glossy and curled on the ground in a delicate mound. The herd waits around, swishing their tails, shifting on strong haunches, for the foal to get his bearings and start walking—to do what is mapped in his genes.

Struggling to stand on wobbly legs, the afterbirth drying on his baby fur, he collapses over and over under his own weight. His thin, spindly legs simply can't get it together. The mares nudge him, trying to help him up, but he is too weak. Then, the dark red stallion approaches. The mares give way for him to, I presumed, help the foal.

Pizza limp in my hand and cheese starting to slide toward the floor, I watched as the stallion very slowly lowers his muzzle to the foal's neck, which is vulnerable and open. And quickly—so quickly that I gasped—he clamps hard onto the foal's neck and sinks his strong and yellowed teeth into the soft flesh. He raises the foal high into the air and violently shakes him back and forth, breaking his neck. The stallion casually drops the foal to the ground and leads the herd away. At the time, I was shocked at the violence of it all. I guess I had some vague sense that animals do this, that their instincts drive them to do things that my human mind, with a tendency at the time to anthropomorphize animals like in the movies and cowgirl narratives I had consumed growing up, didn't understand.

I didn't comprehend at that time, or during my years with Shoshona, that instinct and survival mean everything to horses. They are prey animals after all, and despite the years of domestication worn on their bodies and nestled in their minds, the necessity of survival still drives them. That stallion did what he had to do to protect the herd, and the herd trusted him enough to follow when he led it away. I didn't understand this with Shoshona, but I do now, years later, with Treasure. I'm aware of the obvious falseness of the arrangement between Treasure and me, of the complicated truth that despite my efforts to provide gentle leadership, I am still functioning within a system of domestication. I cannot avoid the fact that in order to develop a relationship that resembles mutuality, as well as to ride safely, I must do things differently than I did with Shoshona or Cody. I've come to believe that horsemanship techniques like those taught by Harry are the only way I can do that without harming Treasure's integrity. They are the only way I can wade through this murky territory and come out feeling okay with myself, with the way I've treated Treasure.

Riding Treasure around Harry's arena, listening carefully as Harry called out to me from where he sat with the women watching intently from beneath their hats that protected them from the desert sun, I tried to remain focused on my energy. I concentrated on the messages I was sending through the reins, through the way my body moved—communicating carefully and understanding that the message suspended between us mattered. I watched Treasure's ears, usually a good indicator of where he was mentally—gently sloping when he was relaxed and present, hard-looking with their curves pointed straight forward when he was distracted—lost somewhere in the distance.

Feeling by the crookedness in his body that Treasure's mind was drifting toward a chipmunk in a nearby wood pile, I trotted him in a small circle, trying to get him with me, to find that moment when his eye would look around the corner and his head would relax and lower as he let go of the thought. But he was pushing through me, eager to remain fixed outside of the arena, far away from me. Noticing I was about to give up, Harry called out to me, "Ashley, if you accept that, you're teaching him to ignore you. You're teaching him that what you are asking doesn't matter, you need to get bigger now." In order to help Treasure look to me for comfort, I had to firm up.

Later that night, as we sat around a small table outside under the dark, wide sky, listening to the buzz of insects and the rustling of the horses in their stalls, I rolled Harry's words around in my mind, weighing what they meant for me—someone who struggles with setting boundaries, in and out of the arena, and not with just Treasure. And I couldn't help but think of Jake, of one particular night a couple of years into our relationship.

Shortly after moving in together, we hosted a party at our house. As a group of us sat around our patio table drinking and smoking cigarettes, the energy shifted. The night was suddenly grim and tense as the group began to bicker about a mutual friend. Alone with him in the house, grabbing a couple of beers from the refrigerator, I asked Jake why he didn't stand up for his friend when everyone was talking badly about him. Jake paused, looked at me coldly, and spat out, "Fuck you, bitch."

It was as if all of the air had been sucked out of my chest, and I tried to form a response through the surprise and hurt as heat spread across my chest and cheeks. Simply turning and walking away was all I could manage in that moment, all I could really do without crying. Upstairs,

I threw Jake's shabby pillow into the hallway before locking the bedroom door with a cool click. The next morning, he knocked tentatively at our bedroom door and I allowed him back in, where he began apologizing profusely.

Somehow, I forgave him, even though I knew in my gut that those words, that resentment and momentary hatred, were a deal breaker—an indicator of times to come. Nonetheless, it seemed easier to forgive than to uproot my life—our life. Yet I knew in my gut that he had chosen that word for a reason, knowing it would hurt me the most, jabbing at my feminism and politics, which he resented so deeply. I told him that he couldn't talk to me like that, but I wasn't surprised when it happened again. And again. I wasn't surprised when he ignored what I asked of him, and the boundaries I tried to set but didn't do the work to keep.

When Jake finally pushed me—an act of physicality I had always suspected he was capable of, an act born of resentment—I wasn't entirely surprised either. But I was afraid. Despite that fear, I continued to live with him for a few more months while I second-guessed my decision to break up with him. Despite already having begun to wander, I struggled with trusting my instincts, and more importantly, I struggled to summon the power to get big enough, and clear enough, to just leave.

—

In the center of the round pen, I stroked Treasure's face from the soft whorl in the middle of his forehead to the bridge of his nose, along the hard permanent ridge and the scar tissue—a constant reminder of the harshness of his former life. He looked at me with his large, sensitive eyes that had been so dull and lackluster when I'd found him. I reached up and unlatched his halter, let it drop from his nose into my fingers, and slung it over my shoulder. Free of restraint, Treasure waited for me to send him out. I pointed in the direction I wanted him to go and wiggled the lead rope at my side. He walked off and turned to move in circles around me.

Walking with my shoulder parallel to his tail, I guided his movements with my own body and energy, speeding up, taking longer strides when I wanted him to move faster into a trot or canter. As he galloped around me, his eye watched, waiting for my cues, for the information that traveled between us. Muscles rippled under his shimmering brown coat; veins bulged across his shoulders toward his thin and graceful legs. I slowed my pace, my breathing, my energy, and Treasure fell from a gallop into a steady trot and finally into a smooth walk. When I stopped, he turned in toward me and walked back into the center, where I stroked his neck and shoulders and rubbed between his ears.

Treasure is too tall for me to mount from the ground, so I lined him up with the fence and climbed on from there. I was careful to watch his ears and eyes to be sure his focus was on me, so he wouldn't spook while I was halfway between the fence and the saddle. Once I was settled in the saddle, balanced and centered, we started off. I kept my own mind focused, constantly seeking the ideal movement, free and forward, that prevented Treasure from getting stuck in his worries. Nothing we do lacks meaning. Each movement I make on each ride has a message and a purpose. I'm hoping that as a result of our work, Treasure will be surer in mind and feet, will be a safe and trustworthy mount, one I can count on because of his willing participation and the removal of force, fear, domination, and resentment from our relationship.

I slid off Treasure's back, my boots landing on the ground with a quick thud. "Now I can see why you like this horse so much, why you keep him around," Harry said. And I could see in the faces of the other women that we had finally gotten it—that we, if just for those few moments in the arena, were partners. This exploration of horsemanship is complicated, and I know that no matter how hard I try, I may never make sense of it all. But in that moment with Treasure, I inched closer.

Crossing the desert once more on the drive home, Candace and I discussed how challenging it was to be really clear about what we were asking of our horses and to find the energy and clarity to react when they ignored us or pushed through the boundaries we had set for them. "I find it so difficult to get really big with

Treasure," I said to Candace, "to get his attention. It's just not how I am." As she drove, I could see her considering this before finally saying what we both already knew: As women, we are expected to be quiet and friendly, not assertive and crystal clear about what we want. Candace told me that we have to learn this with our horses, and that in doing so we will be strengthened. She reminded me that no matter what happens in our lives, when we work with our horses, we practice being assertive and big.

I nodded as she spoke, understanding exactly what she meant. I had experienced it. It was what had first attracted me to this new approach to horsemanship; it is what continues to attract me to horses. It's the only space I've found where I'm rewarded for being firm and confident, with a partnership that leaves me feeling capable and satisfied, at home in my own body, closer to myself and another living, moving, pulsing being. This is something we women rarely see outside of the arena. 🐎

Cody

THE HOSPITAL PLAYED smooth jazz in the chilly operating room. The surgeon fluttered about, preparing himself and chatting with the anesthesiologist, while a nurse helped me climb onto the icy metal table. As we situated the IV tubes and my loose hospital gown, the surgeon reassured me that the procedure would be quick and safe, but the very idea of having cement injected into my spine seemed crude, leaving me deeply uneasy. But I didn't have many options, and I certainly couldn't get back on a horse until my spine was more stable.

I awoke in a room lined with hospital beds, several filled by others working to shake off the fuzz of anesthesia. When the surgeon came to check on me, the first question I asked was whether or not I was cleared to ride again. He chuckled: "Take it easy the next forty-eight hours, but after that you can return to normal activities." In that drugged state, I was confident and sure I'd return to riding seamlessly. However, once the painkillers wore off, the situation was far less simple. In twenty years of riding and putting myself on some risky horses, this was my first serious fall, and from a horse who was far from conventionally unsafe.

When Cody threw me, I was sure I would die. As I sailed through the air, unable to break my fall with my arms or any twist of my body, death seemed inevitable. The thought was a flash of certainty. Throughout my riding career, stories had circulated of broken bones, smashed skulls, riders being dragged by their spooked horses, and fatalities. Soon, mine joined the parade of cautionary tales marching through my head. The first night home from the hospital, I set my alarm clock for every hour, just as the emergency-room doctor had instructed, in case of a concussion. My brother, whom I lived with at the time, checked in on me occasionally as I nestled into the couch to watch television. Zoned out on Norco, I felt a dull worry residing beneath the haze, one I tried to ignore.

After my brother had fallen asleep, the house had grown silent, and the text messages from friends had stopped lighting up my phone, I was forced to consider what my fall had meant for me as a horsewoman. I could no longer brush it off as a fluke like I had in the truck with Jennifer. It was good to be at home and comfortable, with the cool calm of aloneness filling the house. These emotions were amplified by the freedom to doze at all hours, to graze on snacks and sip Diet Dr. Peppers, to watch dramatic movies because it hurt my ribs too much to laugh. Nonetheless, the aloneness also meant that there were few distractions. Each movement and the accompanying pain reminded me of how close I'd come to disaster. And it made me wonder not so much when as *whether* I'd get back in the saddle.

My father asked me not to ride again. He repeated the horror stories already crawling through my head. He began with the one most well-known to him—Christopher Reeve, who was paralyzed after falling headfirst from his horse in a jumping accident. Next, my father reminded me of a customer he'd done work for in the past. The man's boot had become stuck in the stirrup of the saddle when he fell from the horse he was riding. Scared, the horse took off, dragging the man and managing to step on his head repeatedly in the process. Hours had passed before someone found him.

I recalled that a girl at my college had been crushed by the horse she rode on campus. The girl and her friend, members of the university's equestrian team, had been seeking a trail through the campus orchards. In order to avoid heavy university traffic, the girls and their horses took a shortcut that forced them to pass by the university's dairy unit. Cows were lingering near the fence. The girl's horse, having never seen a cow before, spooked and bolted, like many horses when confronted with the unknown. In her attempts to stop her mare, the girl turned her in a circle. But the mare's leg gave out, causing her to collapse on top of the girl, who died of head injuries after three days. The girl came from a horse-loving family, and two years later, her sister also died in a horseback-riding accident when her horse stumbled at a jump, throwing her over his shoulder. This too is the story of the cowgirl, beginning with women like Bonnie McCarroll, whose death was cited as a reason to ban women from rodeos.

———

In high school, I was jumped by a group of girls I didn't know. They came from behind while I was at my locker. Sitting in the counselor's office, I listened to him and my mother discuss the situation. "She deals with thousand-pound animals," my mother told the counselor. "If she wanted to hurt somebody, she would." I didn't believe it myself but felt oddly comforted by the fact that my mother seemed to. When they had finished speaking, the counselor called me in. "If you see the group of girls approach you, just run, get out of there," he said. "That's how they fight." I nodded back at him, not venturing to ask where exactly I was supposed to run to. He told me to go to the bathroom with a partner and to walk in a group to and from my classes.

Although my friends enjoyed the excitement of walking me to class and cute boys eagerly filled the role of protector, their presence did nothing to alleviate the sense of complete helplessness that I was experiencing. Simply existing made me feel exposed and vulnerable in the world. The only thing that evoked safety and peace, and power in my own body—in my own physicality— was riding Shoshona. I felt strong while I was on her; in order to ride well, you need to be. And I felt safe in the world. We often struck out toward the orchards and canals behind my house. Meandering through the orchards drizzling little pink blossoms upon us, inhaling the smell of the peaches merged with the soil after dropping from the trees, and feeling Shoshona's muscles shift beneath me with each step allowed me the chance to learn about independence as did the heroines in the stories I had written so many years prior. I worried that to give up trail riding after my fall was to give up on that part of myself and of my past that seemed integral to who I am today.

—

Jennifer had the horses saddled and ready when I arrived for our first ride after recovering from surgery. Cody stood quietly as I ran my hand up and down the white blaze on his forehead and continued down along his neck and shoulder, reconnecting with my old trail friend. Lifting myself into the saddle, I was hyper-aware of my body and of Cody's. As we rode down the trail from Jennifer's house propped up on the mountain, I worked hard to keep myself present, to block the thoughts about the fall and all of the potential falls that could await me. The trees lining the dusty trail shimmered, tufts of leaves bobbing above us. As we approached the mossy-green lake, where a woman was walking with her three children, the children asked if they could pet our horses.

Glancing up from observing the little boy petting Cody, I saw a truck creep toward us, pulling a trailer carrying a rusty aluminum boat. Jennifer told the woman and her children to move out of the way in case the horses spooked at the noise. As they scurried away, I steadied and planted myself in the saddle, prepared for Cody to bolt. I tipped Cody's head so he could see the truck approaching and where the strange, hollow rumbling originated. Cody's body tensed, his muscles tightly constricted under me, but he remained still as the truck passed. Relieved, I rubbed his neck. But while we remained there, commenting on how well the horses had done, the truck turned around and headed in our direction once again.

Jennifer panicked and rushed forward, riding uphill into the dense trees on the other side of the road. Cody and I followed, which meant the truck and the unusual thundering noise called from behind us. Cody couldn't see it anymore, which amplified the pulsing fear I could already sense building in him, causing his neck and shoulders to brace and tense up. My own fear began to surge through my body—heart pounding, hands trembling. I considered jumping out of the saddle, reasoning that if Cody spooked and bolted uphill, I would fare better on the ground. But the growling of the truck and aluminum boat below us faded away. We made it through the first trail ride since the fall without major incident, yet I was still troubled as I unsaddled and brushed away the sweat and dirt from Cody's coat. Jennifer saw it as a triumph—getting back in the saddle and out on the trail together again. But I couldn't reciprocate the excitement no matter how hard I tried. I was still deeply afraid.

I had never before understood riding to be dangerous in the way that I do now. Candace refers to Treasure as a Labrador in a horse's body because he loves to be around people, which is rare for a retired racehorse after a life of bullying and abuse. Another woman at the ranch once said he was always in my pocket because he's always watching me, following my movements, curious about everything. At the same time, Treasure's sheer power is palpable and reminds me of the fall in a very visceral way at times, such as when I see him out to pasture, running at full speed, faster than any of the other horses, his head swinging side to side as he scans all around him.

I observe that power most sharply when I am riding and something scares him, particularly on our rides through the orchards behind the ranch that constantly buzz with strange sounds of cars, water trickling, and trees humming in the wind. I can feel the fear charged beneath me, can hear his breathing change from steady inhalations and exhalations to hard snorts. But I'm also trying to learn how to guide him forward through what scares him, to offer support, both physically and mentally, to give him space to search for answers. Maybe I need to sense his power in such nuanced ways in order to understand and remember that these creatures are constantly pulsating with instinct, fear, strength, and attachment—features of their nature that I wasn't aware of in Shoshona when I was young.

Practicing a gentler horsemanship, or what writer Tom Moates calls "honest horsemanship," allows me to establish a partnership with Treasure while leaving room for these feelings to exist. In fact, Moates writes, "Physical control over the horse in place of mental companionship and understanding only confines the horse to fewer choices" (27). Gentler horsemanship emphasizes working with a horse's instincts and emotions, keeping their integrity intact as best we can. It leaves room for their fear, so long as we commit to consistently helping them get to a place that is without worry.

Part of my work with Treasure involves building his confidence, which is badly shaken after years of stress on the racetrack. Often, I lead him along the narrow farm road between the ranch and the peach orchards and orange groves. My purpose is to expose him to things that might be scary and allow him the opportunity to keep focused, to show him he can move through and past what may be intimidating and still be okay. As we walk from the hitching post, I am careful to keep his thought with me, his eye on me, his body straight. I am offering support through my body and physical presence. Maintaining a calm, steady stride, we pass the large bush trembling with small birds. Treasure's ears tip forward and his eye strains to see. I ask him to come back, to soften, before continuing onward.

Turning right onto the old, beaten road, Treasure is steady and settled, curious but confident, his stride long and easy. We are alone on the road. To our left, the peach trees are thin—bare skeletons; to our right, horses in pasture watch us intently. Two cows with sad-looking eyes and full faces lift their heads from the grass. Treasure's gait creates a rhythmic clicking each time his hooves meet the worn asphalt. At the end of the road, the orange groves begin. The trees have been uprooted, tipped onto their sides, to be replaced for a new growing season. The dying leaves, crinkled and dry, are dropping into the mud. Treasure, with my support and guidance, stays mostly calm amid the shadowy rows of trees, their twisted limbs splayed out, stretching toward the next overturned tree. I caress the downy fur between his ears—his favorite place to be rubbed. He licks and chews—an indication of contentment in horses. His head stays lowered.

As peaceful as it is on our walks, the sinister some-times creeps up beside us. It can lurk in the shadows of the rows, when all I want to see is the bright fruit peeking through the webs of woody arms and leaves. Recently, a large red truck crawled up the ranch driveway and stopped next to where I was standing. A small dog poked his pinched face out of the window as a woman in sunglasses leaned across the seat. "Has the sheriff stopped by?" she asked. She explained that a robbery had occurred only a half-mile away, and the man had escaped and was last seen running in the direction of the ranch. She said that he was wearing black and brown clothing and could be hiding in the orchards, flat on his stomach, trying to blend in with the dirt and trees. Or he might still be running, attempting to cut through the trees and the pastures, away from the scene of the crime. Within minutes, a helicopter buzzed low over the horses and trees, scanning the area, searching for the man in brown and black. Later that night, I watched the news hoping for resolution, but there was nothing about the man in the orchards.

On our walks, when thoughts of danger threaten our quiet pleasure, I sometimes wonder what I would do should a man step out from behind the trees, perhaps with a knife that glints in the sunlight, that cuts through the leaves. He threatens me, tells me I must come with him or, worse, attacks right there. Other times, I imagine men in a truck using the road as a shortcut, spotting a girl alone with her horse and seizing their opportunity.

I trusted Shoshona to protect me, to allow me to gallop from danger. When a large Rottweiler suddenly appeared from behind an abandoned shed and charged at us, growling and revealing sharp and bright white teeth, I was terrified. As the dog ducked low to bite at Shoshona's thin gray legs, she veered to the left, balancing, before striking with her front right leg at the dog. Her heavy hoof clipped the dog's face, sending him retreating into the trees. Looking back on that moment, I realize that when I was young, I needed Shoshona more than she needed me. Sure, I provided physical sustenance, but that was an effect of domestication and human domination, not something internal that she inherently *needed*.

Treasure *needs*. From the moment I saw him, I could see the urgent want in the bones protruding from his sides, in the teeth jagged from years of neglect, in his eyes, fearful and quick to show the white. I could never—and would never—expect him to carry me away from danger the way I did Shoshona. It's *my* job to do the rescuing. That is the nature of our relationship, our partnership.

Perhaps, without being aware of it, without yet being able to put it in words, I was drawn to Treasure because he was—and still is—very different from Shoshona. He needs me more than I need him. Maybe, in taking on Treasure, I knew in my gut that it was time to grow up, to realize I couldn't look to a horse to take care of me. To make me. Not anymore. The fall solidified that. It drove into my body, with each crack and ache, that horses are simply animals functioning within a system of domestication, reacting as animals do. And that is enough. 🐎

The Pie, Arizona Pie, and Pilgrim

VELVET DECLARES THAT she is in love with horses. She pines after them in the same way her older sister pines after boys. Set in the late-twenties English countryside, *National Velvet* tells Velvet's story as she trains and competes in the Grand National steeplechase with the help of her equine love-match, The Pie. In nearly every girl-and-horse movie, a horseless girl wishes for a horse of her own until the right one comes along. It's fate when her horse soulmate—who's often wild, abused, or otherwise untamable until they meet their girl—comes along. *National Velvet* is no different. Won in a raffle after his previous owner tired of his unruly behavior, The Pie is destined for Velvet, and she for him. Together, they do what no girl and horse have done before: win the dangerous and grueling Grand National race.

For the 1944 film adaptation of the 1935 story by Enid Bagnold, Elizabeth Taylor, who played Velvet, chose the Thoroughbred who played The Pie because she'd ridden him at her country club. Taylor, who was twelve, rode and trained tirelessly for the role, in the process developing a bond with the horse, who was otherwise quite bristly and who reportedly bit crew members and trainers. Taylor was gifted the horse for her thirteenth birthday. No tale of a girl and her horse would be complete without the crash: After a fall from the horse, Taylor broke her back. But like Velvet, a tumble could not stop Taylor from riding.

In *International Velvet*, the 1978 sequel to the film, starring Tatum O'Neal, we learn that Velvet and The Pie are still together but he's out to pasture and out to stud. The movie focuses on Velvet's niece Sarah, who lives with Velvet and her partner John after Sarah's parents died in a car crash. Sarah falls in love with The Pie's last foal before retirement after she watches the foal's birth. She diligently saves money in hopes of buying him for herself, only to find once she's earned enough that he's been sold. We learn, however, that Velvet has bought him for Sarah. The scene of Sarah and the foal meeting again is straight from a romantic movie—they race toward one another, the music swells, and they embrace. It sounds corny and a little absurd, but I can't knock it because I've been there myself.

Sarah names the foal Arizona Pie, and the two are inseparable, as Velvet and The Pie were. Sarah is passionate about being chosen for the British Olympic team; there's no time for boys or any other kind of distractions. Over the course of the movie, Velvet is curiously and firmly on the ground. We eventually discover that Velvet no longer rides because she "lost her nerve" after a devastating fall that left her barren. This is quite a departure from the Velvet who took spill after spill only to hop back on again as she trained for the Grand National.

The film is largely rote: These movies often reproduce the same storylines and dynamics. But horse-girls will still watch them because they stir in these girls something elemental and dreamy, while horseless girls can live out their hopes for horses of their own—for the otherworldly—on the screen. We love the horse for their freedom, and a horseless girl rewarded for her own wildness is something we don't often find in media in general, even if the cowgirl narrative is rarely treated with the same seriousness as the male-driven Western.

Cowgirl narratives—stories about girls and horses—are often trivialized because even though girls love them, they are one of the few subgenres in which the male gaze, a term coined by the film critic Laura Mulvey, is disrupted. In most cow- or horse-girl movies, the woman is not a sex object used to spur the hero's journey, or the domestic goddess to whom the hero returns; she is the hero, bestowed with agency. Although our cowgirl may take a few lickings, she still comes out on top. At one point, echoing *Wild Hearts Can't Be Broken* almost verbatim, Sarah's trainer even asks her, "You're not going to cry, are you?" Sarah, along with Arizona Pie, faces some setbacks, but thanks to hard work and grit, she makes it to the Olympics.

Once Sarah's there, the pressure is on, and she takes a tumble during her run, which incurs a shoulder injury. In true cowgirl form, she gets back on to finish, getting her team to the finals. The team's unsure if she can compete due to the injury. Sarah begs to ride. Velvet advises, "Be sensible"—an *adult*eration of an advice, coming from the same person who left home with her horse, chopped off her hair, and gave her all in one of the most dangerous horse events. This is not the Velvet we know.

Watching the film, I kept waiting for Velvet's triumphant return to the saddle, but it never comes. Instead, *International Velvet* ends with Sarah getting married to the American Olympic team captain and deciding to stay in the U.S. In the final scene, Sarah and her new husband join Velvet and John on the beach on a surprise visit to present Velvet with Sarah's gold medal, and the film closes with the four walking alongshore in heteronormative bliss. And just like in *Wild Hearts Can't Be Broken*, the viewer never learns what becomes of Arizona Pie. It's as if horse love is squarely in the realm of girlhood and folly, while marriage and children wait around the corner.

Who is the cowgirl without her nerve, without a horse?

—

Tucked beneath the blankets and the dark and the weight of the fact that it was our last night together before he moved across the country to Iowa, my boyfriend Michael and I held hands as we drifted off to sleep. We didn't say much of anything but just slept fitfully, occasionally reaching through the dark for one another. The next morning, I rose early to clean stalls at the ranch, dreading the passing of the day. We'd known about the move since the start of our relationship—since that first night together, our voices carrying us from evening until early morning. But in the quiet hours at the ranch, while scooping and raking methodically, I had no choice but to consider thoroughly what that move would initiate.

From California, we searched for a home that would accommodate both of our dogs—a cozy little house on a tree-lined street—before signing a lease together. We discussed how Treasure and I would cross the many miles with Michael to see Iowa fresh with him and to experience all of the firsts. When that plan fell apart, we found ourselves saying our farewells at the train station instead. I was headed back to Fresno, he to his parents' home to load up the car and set off with his father and sister. I hid the tears behind my sunglasses as he held me tight, and we made promises to do our best to get me to Iowa soon, to iron out all the kinks in scheduling. We'd work hard to plan my own trip with Treasure to join him for good. None of this was without great risk, nor without reservations and a heavy heart on my part.

A few weeks after Michael had settled in Iowa, I flew out to visit him. The hours went by quickly as the distance between us closed, as we got nearer to being in the same time zone, state, and finally city. When I passed through the gate, anxious and vibrating with excitement, I spotted him standing under the glow of the airport's fluorescent lights. He was holding a bouquet of flowers, and tears welled up in his eyes. The week's visit was blissful and seamless as we imagined me living there, as we talked furniture and curtains, restaurants and walking trails. We explored by night and lounged in the wide yard covered in green by day, bathing in the shade of massive trees full of squirrels and birds. It felt good to be there, and the sweet intimacy of the visit to what was simultaneously our home and not our home helped alleviate some of my bitter disappointment in not getting to join him in the move. I saw myself living there in Iowa, and when I sat outside watching the robins dart to and fro, I felt raw, seared by the thought of leaving.

I had never been one to consider moving for love, or to even entertain the thought. Every time Jake brought it up in our five years together, I balked, quickly shutting the thought out of my mind. Shoshona gave me a reason to remain place-bound, but even without her, I wouldn't have moved away with him. Instead, after finishing college, I began applying to graduate programs and to jobs elsewhere. I began focusing on my future, with or without Jake. Mostly, I envisioned it without him, knowing that a future with him would pose a greater risk than I was willing to take. This wasn't so with Michael. And the fact that I sat in the shade of his yard imagining myself there every day, without the need for an escape plan, without alternatives, was significant.

—

When I was young, I owned a book called *Princess Smartypants*. The brightly illustrated cover showed our eponymous heroine on a motorcycle, her long blond hair flowing and topped with a delicate tiara. Behind her was a small reptile, one of the many pets she surrounded herself with, along for the ride. In the story, Princess Smartypants never wants to get married; she'd much rather live in her castle with her pets and no husband to answer to. When her parents insist that she marry, she takes to sabotaging the men who vie for her hand, until one comes along and completes all of the near-impossible tasks she has set. Despite his success, however, the suitor does not win her hand. He is instead turned into a frog, and Princess Smartypants gets what she truly wants: to live alone with her pets happily ever after.

The cowgirl narratives I grew up with aren't only about women opting out and choosing to live alone with their pets like Princess Smartypants. Some certainly have elements of romantic love, but these aren't at the forefront. Mostly, the girls roam and have adventures with their horses. Alone. We don't always learn what they grow into . . . until Velvet, that is.

In reality, I've become accustomed to the idea of living a version of these narratives as I've grown more immersed with the horsewomen around me and more at home in my identity as a horsewoman. Drawing partly from their experiences and partly from my own, I can see that I had few choices when men in my past resented the space taken up by horses. Although I recognized that it might seem a cold and solitary existence, I imagined myself living on a ranch, surrounded by horses, free and open and quite possibly alone.

One unifying element in all of the narratives I consumed that strongly influenced my view of relationships was that if something stopped being right and didn't feel like home anymore, I could climb in the saddle and gallop away. Though I was not always good at knowing when to take flight, I knew that as soon as I needed to, I could and would live happily ever after like Princess Smartypants.

The cowgirl narratives that I held dear for so long often intersect with the feminist narratives and research I am interested in now as an adult, including those I teach my Women's Studies students. I cannot separate my thoughts about girls and horses—about women and nature—from what I teach my students. I think not only about the power that we as women may gain from our equine partners, but also about the problem with a reality in which young women need horses—a powerful representation of our inner connections with nature—to feel strong and safe. To be insulated from the hurts of the world and to recover from them. What does that structure mean for the girls without access to the wide-open spaces or freedom to roam? What is recovery when we are with horses who share that ancient pain with us? What is recovery when we bear it alone?

As I read more on the representation of femininity in our culture and what it means for girls, I'm struck by our obsession with horses in girlhood. I discover a discussion of my beloved Princess Smartypants and this problematic binary we feminists are often faced with: We either live alone or settle for some brute who doesn't do his fair share, who needs to be trained. In her book *Cinderella Ate My Daughter: Dispatches from the Frontlines of the New Girlie-Girl Culture*, Peggy Orenstein argues that she wants something more for her daughter, something more like a partnership. We cowgirls, feminist or not, struggle with this binary, too. Jokes about divorce over horses are rampant among cowgirls.

—

In the year following Michael's move, Candace and I often talked about my joining him. Leaning against hay bales under the shade of the barn, we spoke about the cold of the Midwest, of me missing Michael, of logistics. We spoke of risk. Candace had moved for a man before. She'd packed up her horses and had driven across many states to be with someone she loved. When that proved to be disastrous, she drove them right back. As the year marched on, as the heaviness of being away from Michael grew more burdensome for me, our conversations shifted, especially after our recent trip to Harry Whitney's clinic in Arizona for the third year in a row. As we sat around Harry's dining table, a talented and generous writer I'd had the good fortune to meet at just the right time said to me, "Why don't you just move there and bartend and write?" And in that moment, everything seemed so clear.

It wasn't as though Michael and I hadn't thought of it before. We had, just as we'd agonized over how the move would affect my career. In Fresno, I had an adjunct job teaching Women's Studies, and although I had to bartend to survive, I was still in a classroom. But after a year of still being in the same place I'd been the year before, applying for jobs in Iowa and missing opportunities because I wasn't present to interview or start immediately, the thought of dropping everything to move, of tending bar and writing seemed surprisingly viable, even attractive. I was tired of leading parallel lives. Living between two homes had taken its toll.

When the gray first settled over me, I was crying at the slightest provocation—a song about heartache, an essay, a bird resting on a fencepost—as the tears were always just beneath the surface. I started smoking to settle my churning stomach. I returned to my counselor and shook and shuddered on her couch as I told her of the stress I was under. She said it sounded like I was in mourning. In a lot of ways, I was. I was mourning losing Michael, teaching, and my horsemanship community. I was mourning that all of the elements to make up my perfect life were there but somehow disjointed. Perhaps, in some ways, I was even mourning the sureness of going it alone, the openness of my future, that lonesome bit in my heart that was certain men would let me down. I was suddenly at a point where I had to leave all of that behind and move on. Although moving on was good, even pleasurable, there was something uncomfortable in it, too.

Of course, Treasure weighed heavy on my mind in all of this. I needed him more than ever as I struggled to find my bearings in the world. The irony was not lost on me, and I marveled at how he'd come to me in a state very much like my own—in a gray space, lacking clarity, quivering with anxiety. He needed me so desperately in those early days, and suddenly, it was I who had no real sense of the world. Often, when Harry talks about getting big, he describes knowing what you want before you ask for it. One of the biggest challenges I had in working with Treasure was being clear with him, mostly because I was just so hopelessly unclear about what I wanted. I left him hanging, worried, while I fumbled around.

After years of working on getting bigger, after recovering from my fall as a horsewoman, both physically and symbolically, I am more certain in my work with Treasure, although I still have so far to go. He is no longer living in this gray space as our communication has improved, has grown more precise. I, on the other hand, still occupy it, and I cannot help but think about the strangeness of this shift.

I came to think of it in more pronounced ways at Harry's most recent clinic, where I was forced to confront the fear that I'd been carrying around and that I'd been unable to fully shake off in the years following the fall no matter how hard I tried. In the arena, Treasure and I completed a few calm and smooth circles, despite the violent desert wind ripping around us. Bushes shook and the wind howled, but Treasure remained unfazed. It was obvious we'd gotten far from where we were at the start of this journey in horsemanship and rehabilitation, at the start of our relationship. I felt proud of our good work. But when Harry suggested I ride Treasure outside of the arena, the confidence drained from me. The thought was terrifying. Between my fear of trail riding after the fall and the unpredictable weather, the idea of moving beyond the safety of the controlled arena left a pit in my stomach. Yet I knew that setting out into the unknown was critical. I knew Treasure was ready.

Hesitantly, I nudged Treasure along. I lined him up to the gate and reached down to unlatch it with a shaky hand as I gripped the reins with the other. With those first few steps outside of the arena, my heart raced and my hand found its way toward Treasure's neck, where I buried my fingers in his mane. Logically, I had no reason to be afraid, but my body still responded with the bone-deep fear that had taken hold after the fall. It was difficult to explain to the other women at the clinic what I was so scared of; I found myself hedging, using phrases like "muscle memory" to suggest that the anxiety was beyond my control. I wasn't afraid of Treasure spooking; it was something different. More and more, it seemed to be a fear of the unknown, that unknowable, unforeseen terror—the accident, the crash, the fall that I could not anticipate—that no amount of athleticism or skill could protect me from.

The closest thing I could compare it to was my experience after being mugged. Jake and I were walking home late one night when three young men and a woman attacked from behind. The woman swung hard and hit me in the back of the head with such force that I nearly fell on my face, while one of the men grabbed my purse and raced down the street, leaving me with the others. Stunned, I realized that the woman was still trying to hit me. I stumbled backward to avoid her swings, but I didn't run, didn't fight back. I was frozen, stupefied, staring at the muggers before catching up to Jake, who'd left me behind to chase the boy with my purse.

After that, just sensing someone approach me from behind sent a shiver down my spine and caused my body to tense up. It was as though my body was certain, in spite of reason suggesting otherwise, that I was going to be attacked again. Though I told myself over and over that I was safe, particularly as the fear would take hold in embarrassing ways—at work, school, the grocery store—my body still reacted this way for years. The same is true of my fear after the fall. And on that day out at Harry's, on my first ride in the open desert without the comfort of the others and their horses, it took hold just as furiously as it had so many times before.

Harry urged us on, encouraging me to move Treasure forward, to keep him with me. And although I was afraid, I did. Treasure took long strides toward the barn that rattled and shook in the wind, and we made our way around it. Walking toward the others, who waited for us back at the arena, I felt exhilarated yet exhausted. Depleted. The week went on like this. Each day, Harry pushed us—pushed me—further into the unknown until finally, we were traipsing into the wash, through the ocotillo bushes that reached across the wide, wide desert. We trotted up and down the sandy washes and hills. We were unstoppable, Treasure and I.

With each step toward what scared me, toward the unnamable disasters ahead, the fear lifted. I felt weightless for the first time in a while. Healed. I had dreamed of doing this with Treasure from the moment he came into my life, and for years, I was too afraid to actually do it. Fatigued after a week of such extreme fear and relief, I sat staring out the window on the car ride home and considering how far Treasure and I had come, how far we still had to go, and how badly I needed this clinic. Perhaps, I thought, I'm ready to move toward the unknown in other areas, too.

—

In the past, when I fantasized about moving, I would be hauling Treasure alone, crossing the country—to anywhere—in our solitude. Treasure and I would pack up like nomads and roam together across miles of empty road, my hair whipping in the wind, music blaring from the radio. I remember reading that when horses and humans were more tightly linked, they moved together, but as humans collected more goods to weigh them down, they also grew more place-bound and no longer moved so freely. Wheels and carts became integral; so did money. To move now, you have to really mean it. For all the freedom and movement that horses represent, those who care for horses in the twenty-first century are more place-bound than their horse-loving ancestors ever were. Picking up and moving to join Michael, and taking the risk of setting out with no job or money, simply would not work with Treasure in tow.

One morning shortly after our return from Harry's clinic, while Candace and I were talking under the eaves of the barn as we always did, she brought up my moving. "Just leave Treasure here," she said. "He's happy, he's in a good place, just go on ahead. He can stay here as long as you need or want. Go out there and write." With that, the road to Michael—a new path to a new future and opportunities—opened up. I felt brave and renewed with this wide future ahead, as though I could explore sides of myself I hadn't fully realized yet. However, I was also apprehensive about what moving ahead of Treasure would mean for me. For us.

With Candace's willingness to care for Treasure, I was free to go and find a job, to carve out a place in the world for Treasure and me. This was easier said than done, however, and it didn't answer the question of whether I was prepared for life without Treasure, no matter how temporary. The longest I'd gone without him was a month and a half, when he went to live with Shea for training and craniosacral therapy. Even then, I could visit. In the days leading up to my move, I spent as much time with Treasure as possible, as though I could store up the feelings of peace and strength he and the ranch inspired. Time slowed when we were in the arena together. I always enjoyed my time with Treasure, even when it was deeply challenging; I savored those moments. And on our final night before my move, we had a ride straight out of the cowgirl movies.

I arrived in the late evening after a tiring day of preparing to move. The barn was quiet. All of the horses had been turned out for the night, and there was no sign of Candace. As I walked out to get Treasure, I noticed that Candace's horse was in the arena, which posed a problem. I couldn't ride in the arena with her horse out there, and I didn't like the idea of using the small round pen for my last ride with Treasure before the move. One other option remained. I could take Treasure into the open field, lined with rows and rows of rice, out behind the ranch. I'd never ridden there; few did. The horses spooked at the trembling rice stalks and large herons often emerged from the water unexpectedly.

Treasure and I spent a lot of time near the rice fields, but I was always on the ground, lounging in the grass while he grazed lazily in the sun. I didn't even know if I could find anything there to climb on to mount him. As the sun began to slide away, I decided I needed to saddle up and try. I worked him from the ground first. His eyes darted at every new movement and his body was tense. He rushed through each circle around me, pushing to look at everything he could. I stopped him, moved him in the other direction, backed him: I did anything and everything to get his mind on me and away from the concern about his surroundings. With this, his muscles relaxed, his head lowered, and his eyes softened.

Scanning the field, I found nothing sturdy or high enough to act as a mounting block, so I lifted my foot into the stirrup and shimmied my way up his tall body and into the saddle. Treasure stood still while I did this, patiently putting up with my complete lack of grace. As the evening settled in, we began moving around the large, open field, trotting and walking, swiftly moving in circles large and small, right and left. The sky was deepening quickly, turning pink, and I knew that soon I'd have to dismount.

Treasure's movements were forward and sure, and as he moved into the trot, he offered a gallop. As the sun set, Treasure and I galloped through that final evening together, beautiful and intimate. Tears welled up in my eyes, because I could not have asked him for a better final ride. As we stood in the center of the field watching the shadows lengthen across the dirt, my thoughts returned again to how far Treasure—and I—had come in our four years together. I knew that he was ready to move on with me once I'd blazed a trail for us in Iowa: that once I'd planted some roots, he'd join me.

This, too, was easier said than done. Michael and I finally decided that we couldn't keep living apart and needed to make the move happen, that a job—any job— would follow. I felt sure it would work. I knew that if I hurried, I could easily pick up a bartending job once the semester ended and all the students headed back home, leaving openings that had to be filled. I knew my family would help me move. My friend Kim joined me on the drive to help with my dog, my cat, and the many lonely miles. Within a couple of weeks in Iowa, I'd somehow landed my dream job with a farmed animal rescue organization and had some part-time teaching work. Michael and I had everything we wanted, which felt charmed.

But Treasure was still missing and until he joined me, all would feel incomplete. The business of filling my time without him was tricky. As Kim and I drove through desolate Nevada, the lush hills of Utah, and rugged Nebraska, I envisioned a number of hobbies that I might enjoy. I imagined taking yoga classes and spending my evenings finding inner peace and greater health, or going on bicycle rides and riding countless miles with the wind in my hair. Eventually, we crossed into the broad emerald of Iowa, and all of those versions of me lost their luster. It was as though I'd left a piece of myself behind, and the loss hit me like a phantom limb. In Iowa, such feelings could come on at any time. In the dark and quiet moments before bed, or as I watched the rabbits race through the grass, my mind would wander to Treasure. At times, I couldn't even mention his name without crying. No one else could make me feel as powerful in the world.

On my first visit back to California, I went straight to see Treasure. As I drove down the dirt road, I immediately spotted him in the pasture grazing. When I got to the barn, a few pastures from where Treasure stood, I called out hello to someone. Upon hearing my voice, Treasure's head shot up, and he raced across the pasture to the gate. I sped over to him, seized and overwhelmed with emotion. Like Sarah and Arizona Pie, we locked in an embrace. I ran my hands over his neck, tears streaming down my face. There it was: my heart, my identity, my strength, my soul.

—

In both *National Velvet* and *International Velvet*, as in most cowgirl narratives, the women profess their abiding love for their horses. Yet, the horses are rarely seen. The horses give of their bodies—in fact, Velvet even proclaims that The Pie would "burst his heart" for her—but that devotion is always portrayed as what they want or need to do. Rarely do we linger on the horses, and certainly never on their thoughts, to examine whether this is true. The closest we come to something akin to a horse's perspective is in the 1998 film *The Horse Whisperer* (based on the 1995 novel of the same name). That that perspective is honored is largely because the main character is inspired by horsemanship practitioners Tom Dorrance, Ray Hunt, and Buck Brannaman.

In the film, after a tragic and traumatizing accident, Grace and her horse Pilgrim are left reeling. Annie, Grace's mother, knows she must act and hauls them from New York to Montana to work with "horse whisperer" Tom Booker. In several scenes, Tom appears to see Pilgrim for who he is and for where he is emotionally, which is unique in cowgirl fiction and nearly nonexistent in the hyper-masculine cowboy fiction. Grace is seen, too. Then, of course, come scenes in which cows and calves are roped and branded. Grace is drawn in to help. It is, in fact, part of Grace's transformation. How can one animal be seen so clearly while another is not?

Beyond the love story that develops between Annie and Tom is that of Grace and Pilgrim reconnecting after their accident. As I watch the film again, tears well up in my eyes. The ultimate scene is when Tom begins teaching Pilgrim to lie down so Grace can mount him. Pilgrim, troubled by this, struggles, and Grace wants to stop. Tom pushes on, eventually getting Pilgrim to the other side. Now, normally, a responsible horsemanship trainer would do this kind of thing slowly and sparingly, but for narrative's sake, the training moves quickly. Soon, Grace is back in the saddle with the help of Pilgrim. They trot and gallop around the ring. Grace shoots both arms in the air, triumphant, and she rubs her horse's neck. She's found her nerve again, and the horse being in a good place mentally is instrumental. I had to learn this with Treasure, that one cannot resurrect the fearless girl without the horse. It's why I couldn't do it with Cody.

So often when the horse is exalted as our symbol of power and freedom, they themselves are lost. Lost to our ambition, to sport, to slaughter. Alice Walker delves into this in her essay "Am I Blue," meditating on what humans have wrought upon the horse's nature. She writes, "And I thought, yes, the animals are forced to become for us merely 'images' of what they once so beautifully expressed." It is why we may look at a racehorse—with a jockey hanging upon their face as though waterskiing, foam dripping from their mouth, their eyes frantic— and think, "It's beautiful, this sport of kings." We have lost our ability to communicate with the horse the way we could when we were kids, when communing with animals came more easily, and we fail to acknowledge what is right in front of us. I'm guilty of it, too.

There are so many reasons to love and respect the cowgirl, to want to channel her power through the horse, but we've got to see the dark with the light. This includes reckoning with her dark history of colonization, her move from wild woman to anesthetized rodeo queen. For white cowgirls, it means understanding that alongside the cowgirls we know like Bonnie McCarroll were the Black, Indigenous, and all women of color who have been whitewashed out of rodeo. It means understanding that the movies belie the truth about horse industries. Take *National Velvet*. Behind the heartwarming story of triumph—an important message for many girls—is the truth about the Grand National and other events like it, where equine injury and death are not only common but unsurprising.

When we talk of synchrony with our horses, we can reach this synchrony more authentically with a full and clear picture of where the cowgirl came from and where she needs to go to truly respect the horse, who gives us the world despite us giving them so little in return. Our horses gird us against what oppresses us, offering us a dose of magic each time they allow us on their backs. They carry us through places that are scary, figuratively and literally, and give us the power to make that journey. Let us only see them. And perhaps this is what can happen when the cowgirl grows up, when the stories catch up to real life, when life inside the arena begins to truly bleed into life outside of it, and when the fear and risk take on a new form and shade. Perhaps this is what can happen when the old stories are outgrown and cast off and a new narrative emerges. 🐎

Acknowledgments

THANK YOU TO Martin Rowe and Lantern for giving this project a home. This book started in my MFA program, where I found inspiration and tireless support from my thesis advisors John Hales, Steven Church, and Linnea Alexander. Thank you all for nurturing my writing practice. I look back fondly at my time in graduate school because of your steadfast guidance. Thank you to California State University, Fresno, for granting me the Graduate Student Research and Creative Support Award, which contributed to some of my horsemanship activities. I appreciate the insightful feedback from writers Maggie Nelson and Alison Hawthorne Deming, whom I had the good fortune of working with at the Tin House Writer's Workshop and the Orion Bread Loaf Environmental Writers Workshop respectively. Thank you to *Connotation Press* and *Bitch* magazine for publishing essays and blog posts that have grown into chapters for this book.

Thank you to my writing group—Bevin O'Connor, Stephanie Tsank, and Wayne Anderson. I so enjoy eating fries and writing with you.

I wrote this book at the beginning of my horsemanship education, and in the time since, I've continued to seek knowledge and grapple with my own shortcomings. I owe immense gratitude to those in the horsemanship community whose talents, grace, and wisdom continue to challenge me in the best possible ways: Shea Stewart, Harry Whitney, Gail Ivey, and Ross Jacobs. I can't say enough about Harry Whitney's generous spirit, and each chance I get to watch him work with horses is a blessing. Thank you to the horsewomen, from California to Iowa, who have shared this passion with me, especially Sara Etter who has also generously shared her horse, Rain. Deepest thanks to Treasure, who has my whole heart.

Thank you to my friends and family, who have encouraged me each step of the way. From the time I wrote detective stories and carried them around in a briefcase, my family has fostered my creativity. This book would not have been possible without my mother and aunt Erika, who gave me the love of a gray mare. Rilo, my fluffy canine companion, you bring me great joy every single day. Thank you to my husband, Michael, for your unconditional love and for the gift of time, which helped this book to take shape.

Bibliography

All URLs accessed June 17, 2020

Burbick, Joan. *Rodeo Queens and the American Dream*. New York: PublicAffairs, 2002.

Couturier, Lisa. "Dark Horse." *Orion* 29, no. 4 (2010). https://orionmagazine.org/article/dark-horse/.

Holbrook Pierson, Melissa. *Dark Horses and Black Beauties: Animals, Women, A Passion*. New York: W. W. Norton, 2001.

Jacobs, Ross (Good Horsemanship – Ross Jacobs). "From time to time I get asked if I think horses can enjoy work…." Facebook, August 6, 2019. https://www.facebook.com/permalink.php?story_fbid=1926735014093625&id=275719312528545&tn=K-R.

———. "I was looking for an old email with…." Facebook, February 17, 2020. https://www.facebook.com/permalink.php?story_fbid=2288739524559837&id=275719312528545.

Kent, Bill. "'The Horse Was in Charge.'" *The New York Times*, May 4, 1997.

King, Ynestra. "The Ecology of Feminism and the Feminism of Ecology." In *Feminist Theory: A Reader*, edited by Wendy K. Kolmar and Frances Bartkowski, 469–474. New York: McGraw Hill, 2005.

"Listen to America." *Huffington Post*, September 27, 2018. Video, 9:41. https://www.youtube.com/watch?v=p6ofyT0V4mg.

Merchant, Carolyn. *The Death of Nature: Women, Ecology, and the Scientific Revolution.* New York: Harper & Row, 1983.

Moates, Tom. *A Horse's Thought: A Journey into Honest Horsemanship.* Floyd, VA: Spinning Sevens Press, 2008.

Orenstein, Peggy. *Cinderella Ate My Daughter: Dispatches from the Frontlines of the New Girlie-Girl Culture.* New York: Harper Collins, 2011.

Sewell, Anna. *Black Beauty.* New York: JM Dent & Sons, 1921.

Walker, Alice. "Am I Blue? Ain't These Tears in These Eyes Tellin' You?" *Ms. Magazine*, no. 15 (November 1986): 29.

About the Author

Photo credit: Dawn Frary

ASHLEY WELLS is a writer living in Logan, Utah where she teaches in the English Department at Utah State University. She teaches courses in rhetoric and composition, including one on the rhetoric of cowgirls and freedom. Her work exploring cowgirl narratives has appeared in *Bitch* magazine, *Connotation Press*, and *Jezebel*. Wells earned her Master of Fine Arts degree in Creative Writing Nonfiction from California State University, Fresno.

About {bio}graphies

The {bio}graphies series explores the relationships between human and nonhuman animals through scholarship in the humanities, social sciences, and natural sciences viewed through the lens of autobiography and memoir, to deepen and complicate our perspectives on the other beings with whom we share the planet.

About the Publisher

LANTERN PUBLISHING & MEDIA was founded in 2020 to follow and expand on the legacy of Lantern Books—a publishing company started in 1999 on the principles of living with a greater depth and commitment to the preservation of the natural world. Like its predecessor, Lantern Publishing & Media produces books on animal advocacy, veganism, religion, social justice, psychology and family therapy. Lantern is dedicated to printing in the United States on recycled paper and saving resources in our day-to-day operations. Our titles are also available as e-books and audiobooks.

To catch up on Lantern's publishing program, visit us at www.lanternpm.org.

facebook.com/lanternpm
twitter.com/lanternpm
instagram.com/lanternpm